ALSO BY WILLIAM JULY II

*Brothers, Lust and Love: Thoughts on
Manhood, Sex and Romance*

*Understanding the Tin Man: Why So
Many Men Avoid Intimacy*

THE HIDDEN LOVER

What Women Need to
Know That Men Can't Tell Them

THE

HIDDEN

LOVER

William July II

BROADWAY BOOKS
NEW YORK

BROADWAY

Broadway Books titles may be purchsed for business or promotional use or for special sales. For information, please write to: Special Markets Department, Random House, Inc., 1745 Broadway, New York, NY 10019.

PRINTED IN THE UNITED STATES OF AMERICA

BROADWAY BOOKS and its logo, a letter B bisected on the diagonal, are trademarks of Broadway Books, a division of Random House, Inc.

Visit our Web site at www.broadwaybooks.com

First Edition published 2003

Book design by Jennifer Ann Daddio

Library of Congress Cataloging-in-Publication Data
July, William.
The hidden lover: what women need to know that men can't tell them/
William July II—1st ed.
p.   cm.
Includes bibliographical references.
1. Man-woman relationships. 2. Men—Psychology. 3. Self-disclosure.
4. Interpersonal communication. I. Title.
HQ801 J852 2003
306.7—dc21   2003066742

ISBN 0-385-50135-8

1 3 5 7 9 10 8 6 4 2

DEDICATED TO LOVERS—

the world's destiny is in our hands

"Now we see but a poor reflection as in a mirror;

then we shall see face to face. Now I know in part; then

I shall know fully, even as I am fully known."

1 CORINTHIANS 13:12

CONTENTS

ACKNOWLEDGMENTS

First I thank God for flowing creative inspiration through my soul.

To my wife, Jamey, the muse God put into my life: Thank you for keeping me inspired when I'm tired and ready to move to the moon. Truly the woman Solomon spoke of in the book of Proverbs, ". . . more precious than rubies."

Thanks to some of the musicians who oiled my thoughts as they streamed through my mind while writing: Azymuth, for their Brazilian-flavored jazz, the incomparable Steely Dan, Al Jarreau's voical magic, and the late great Grover Washington, Jr.—smoothest of the smooth. It will be another millennium before someone else like Mr. Magic comes along.

More thanks than I can express goes to my mother and father for programming me for success as a child with love, respect and room to grow; and a good "no" when necessary.

A shout out to all of the kids I've taught in the Writers in the Schools Program. I love you all and you've made me very proud!

A big thanks to audiences nationwide at colleges, churches and events who've come out to listen and interact with me at the discussions and lectures.

Thanks to every person who has bought my books. Thank you for keeping me in print! I also thank the bookstores who keep me on the shelves year round.

I can't say enough good things about my editor, the one and only Janet Hill. Truly an original. I believe they broke the mold when they made her. Also a huge thanks to Toisan Craigg and Roberta Spivak, who both invested many hours of hard work into shaping this book. Many, many thanks to my publicity machine, especially Erin Curtin. I also extend a sincere thanks to the many individuals at Doubleday I've never met who make my books successful—the copy editors, people in the mailroom, marketing, the sales force, the legal department, the royalties department and everyone else behind the scenes in taking a book from the thought in my head to bookshelves.

INTRODUCTION

I've devoted a lot of time and energy to the subject of relationships because I'm fascinated by the dynamics that seem
to pull us in and out of one another's lives. That fascination
didn't begin as a carefree hobby, but rather as a quest to discover what relationships meant to me as I constantly went in
and out of them. Those thoughts and reflections then grew
into written expressions from my heart, which eventually
became the books I now write.

   In discovering the lover within, I also discovered many
things about myself as a man and what we perceive to be
manhood in America. Many of the masculine traits we cele-
brate are indeed admirable and important, such as decisive-
ness, single-minded focus, determination, independence and
strength. On the other hand, when these traits are taken to the

extreme and become hyper-masculine distortions, they become self-destructive. When a man becomes hyper masculine, he begins to rot away inside, a process which manifests itself through broken relationships, addictions or overly aggressive behavior. Thinking on these things and talking at length with other men, I began to see how such distortions of manhood work to ruin our relationships with women. Those observations led to my previous book, *Understanding the Tin Man: Why So Many Men Avoid Intimacy.*

Upon completing *Understanding the Tin Man,* I felt there was another dimension to the issue that needed to be discussed at length. There is another type of man similar to the tin man who actually operates exclusively within relationships. Like the tin man, he has problems with intimacy. But unlike the tin man, this man, the "hidden lover," has a different dilemma with intimacy. He isn't avoiding intimacy like the tin man. The hidden lover feels drawn toward intimacy but has trouble making the connection because he feels blocked when it comes to expressing what he feels inside.

That's why this book was written. There are many things that men haven't said to women about how they feel. Most men, despite their stoic exterior, have a full range of feelings operating under the hood. They have passionate feelings and emotions that they may not be expressing to women because they aren't yet comfortable doing so. This book aims to bring some of those issues to the surface.

Bringing those issues to the surface wasn't easy. In doing

my research for this book, I encountered hundreds of women who were more than willing to share their opinions, anecdotes and experiences in relationships. But men, the subject of the book, weren't so forthcoming. In fact, sometimes I felt like Indiana Jones when I was trying to find men who would speak up about the things they wanted women to know. I should clarify that it wasn't difficult to get men to complain about things. But to get men to go to the next level and talk about the fears and vulnerabilities behind those complaints was a different thing altogether.

In an odd way, it was actually funny sometimes. One moment a guy would be brash, outspoken and strongly opinionated. But when I tried to go from general generic issues into more personal subjects, he'd freeze. Getting men to talk about their fears and vulnerabilities in relationships can be like pulling teeth.

On the other hand, there were men who had long been looking for an opportunity to talk about the issues that most affect them emotionally. Those men found my probing to be a release because they wanted to talk about these things. These men had pent-up feelings and emotions to vent, so for them just getting a listening ear was soothing. That's the goal of this book. I want men to get an opportunity to expose their most guarded feelings to women in a safe environment. In turn, I want women to hear some of the fears and vulnerabilities of men without all of the emotions that are usually erupting when a man's feelings finally surface.

My hope is that reading this book will lead men and women into dialogues of their own at the breakfast table or in the bedroom—wherever their discussion needs to take place. To that end, I invite you not only to read this book but also to try the self-exploratory journal exercises at the end of each chapter. I hope you'll find this book a catalyst for your own conversations in helping you reach more fullfillment in your relationships and personal life.

CHAPTER 1

REAL LOVER OR HIDDEN LOVER

Which One Is He?

Lover. It must be one of the most misunderstood and abused words in the English language. Often we take the meaning of "lover" to be only romantic or sexual. But let's take a new look at the word "lover." When we do so, we discover that hidden within that word is a new meaning that we can apply to our relationships to make them better.

First, let's look at the word "love" as defined by Webster's dictionary*:

Love—a profoundly tender, passionate affection for another person. An intense personal attachment or affection.

Love—a devoted attachment or passionate affection for another person.

Note, the word "sex" is nowhere to be found in this definition of the word "love."

*Webster's Revised Unabridged 1996, 1998.

Now let's look at the definition of the suffix "er" as defined by the American Heritage dictionary*:

-er—"one that performs a specified action."

Combining the word "love" with the suffix "er," we get the true definition of the word "lover." To paraphrase, *a real lover is a person who works at a profoundly tender, passionate affection for another person.*

Which brings me to my point and the purpose of this book. The real lover in so many men is hidden behind walls. On the outside, men tend to show their affection through money, gifts, sex or doing things for a woman. Giving in these ways is good, but there is a deeper and more intimate place where women ultimately want to connect with us. Women want to connect with our feelings. That's where the real lover dwells inside of us. But when it comes to sharing the real lover inside, many men are in hiding. Afraid or unwilling to put in the emotional work necessary to make a true connection to a woman. This book sheds light on the reluctance of men to be complete lovers by revealing what so many men are hesitant to discuss and the reasons for the silence. The issue is two-sided, involving both how men relate to women and how women view and relate to men. That's why open and direct communication is needed on this issue—not as a matter of placing blame, but as a realistic and balanced approach to the issues that cause men to "hide" their thoughts and feelings. I hope that through reading this book, women will

*American Heritage Dictionary, 4th Ed., 2000 (Houghton Mifflin).

better understand men. And as for the hidden lover, I hope it helps him take a step toward a "profoundly tender, passionate affection" for his significant other.

EASIER SAID THAN DONE

Being a lover is a 24–7, 365-day-a-year job for which the weak need not apply. It includes running errands, cooking, cleaning, doing things when you want to (and when you don't!), communicating, seeing a woman at her best and her least, helping her, knowing when to just listen and not help. In other words, it requires commitment. Look at the root of the word "commitment" and you find the word "commit." To sum it up, one has to really put himself into the whole of a relationship for it to work, not just the easy parts. Many men (and women) opt out of the work part; they just want the romance, the euphoric highs that come at the beginning. Maybe that's why there are so many people with the title boyfriend, girlfriend, husband and wife, yet not enough of them seem to be lovers. I'll be the first one to tell you that this is easier said than done. But that's where the commitment part comes in.

There are two reasons it's difficult to overcome being a hidden lover. First, one must do an honest self-inventory. We must ask ourselves the hard questions about who we are. Also, we must reflect upon the events and people who contributed to making us who we are. Some people don't want to look at themselves that closely because it isn't usually a very comfortable process. However, this is a step that must be taken. Lack of self-reflection is one of the main reasons we go plunging headfirst into relationship after relationship not knowing what we want or should expect from the other person. Much of the time we don't even know that much about ourselves.

The second obstacle to overcoming being a hidden lover is found in the societal role that men play. The traditional role of men in our society has given us all a mask to wear. The mask of superman: the man who must make big money, have all the power, know the answer to every question, etc. We feel we must be the man who gets a promotion every year at work, repairs the car, balances the checkbook and makes love all night. Starting from the time we are young boys in this society, we're taught that such things are expected of us, and that those things add up to our value as men. So instead of expressing ourselves when we feel the burden is too heavy, we keep a stiff upper lip. We wear the mask hiding how we really feel deep inside, where it burns a hole in our souls.

Yet there's a part of every man that yearns to take off the mask. Inside every hidden lover is a man who would love to have the freedom to be expressive and feel safe enough to share his vulnerabilities. Because this often conflicts with the role he feels he must assume in his relationship, many men rarely express their true emotions, even to the women they love. And as long as that wall is there, a relationship can't reach its highest level.

WHY THERE IS A HIDDEN LOVER INSIDE EVERY MAN

As I mentioned, from the time we are boys we men are taught to hide or suppress our emotions and feelings. Boys are programmed to define manhood by power and achievement. For example, observe some of the games boys play: arm wrestling, hard-hitting tackle football, foot races, wrestling, king of the mountain. Boys are always testing each other to see who is stronger, faster and taller. They're placing their worth in those things. Therefore, it's easy for boys to slip into a mindset that views emotions and feelings as of secondary importance, if not altogether a nuisance. The reality is that men and boys do feel emotions and desire to experience that part of themselves, but unfortunately many of us feel we have to hide them in order to fill the role we perceive as being a man. To put it another way, men and boys learn to hide their humanness deep inside while presenting a game face for the world, a face that shows no emotion or vulnerability. It is that very hiding that creates the hidden lover. *The hidden lover longs for pure open connection, emotionally and spiritually, with his mate.*

Now that I've defined what I mean by the term "hidden lover," I want to elaborate on some of the things that create barriers to intimate connection for hidden lovers.

MAJOR CHALLENGES FACED BY HIDDEN LOVERS

1. Healing from pain in his past so it doesn't ruin his relationship. (See Chapter 3, His Hidden Pain.)
2. Explaining to his significant other why he feels communicating with her can be difficult. (See Chapter 9, Why the Hidden Lover Feels He Can't Really Talk to You.)
3. Learning to feel comfortable asking his significant other for help. (See Chapter 5, The Hidden Lover Needs Your Help but Doesn't Want to Ask for It.)
4. Managing the responsibilities of a relationship without feeling burdened. (See Chapter 6, How Fear of Losing Freedom Affects the Hidden Lover.)
5. His views on sex. (See Chapter 8, The Hidden Lover's Views on Sex: He's Not Like All the Other Guys.)
6. Overcoming rigid old beliefs about manhood that make it difficult for him to overcome being a hidden lover. (See Chapter 4, How Trying to Be Superman Creates a Hidden Lover.)
7. Expressing to his lover that he wants to be appreciated. (See Chapter 7, The Hidden Lover's need for Appreciation and Respect.)

WHY CAN'T MEN JUST TELL WOMEN THESE THINGS?

There are lots of reasons men feel they can't tell women the things that are in this book. Some men don't know how to put these things into words. Some men feel their mate just couldn't handle the truth, that she'd be hurt, overly sensitive or angry if she knew some of the things that are revealed in this book. For those reasons many men feel they should just grin and bear it. They take a "why bother" attitude and keep their feelings inside for the sake of peace. But it's not healthy for a relationship to have issues that are rumbling just below the surface and threatening to ultimately rip things apart. When an issue stands in the way of a couple's growth or cohesiveness, the "why bother" belief will only make the problem worse. It's better to get things out into the open: the good, the bad and the ugly.

I've written some pretty bold things in this book. It rips the cover off political correctness in relationships and dares to expose the raw feelings that men have about some things. Please don't take this as a whine fest or a gripe-a-thon; nor is it intended as a list of excuses men use to avoid being intimate and accountable in relationships. The men who are whiners and gripers are not hidden lovers; they're just lazy and looking for excuses. This book is about the men who want to connect, but have serious and very real obstacles to doing so. To that end, I feel it is necessary to be blunt and, when necessary, to go outside the bounds of political correctness.

IT'S NOT JUST A MALE ISSUE

Anybody, male or female, can be a hidden lover. The issues of the hidden lover have more to do with how people act in a relationship than with their gender. When I was on tour promoting my book *Understanding the Tin Man,* many women told me they were "tin women," which underscored the reality that intimacy issues aren't a problem just for men. These issues have to do with each person's unique life circumstances and experiences. Of course, we don't have to choose to be controlled by our emotional history; we can change. To that end, although this book is addressed toward the issues of men, it also offers an opportunity for healing to the many women who see a hidden lover in themselves as they read this book.

THE HIDDEN LOVER QUIZ

Label the following comments as true or false. Keep a running tally of your "true" responses. Then score yourself on the scale following the quiz.

1. I let my significant other know only about half of

what I'm really feeling.

2. I will never completely open up to my significant other.

3. Honesty is an idealistic goal rather than a day-to-day reality in relationships; sometimes a small lie is better than being truthful.

4. I would rather not tell her something if I think my significant other is going to want to discuss it.

5. I usually avoid arguments with my significant other by avoiding things we disagree on even if it means I don't get to express how I feel.

6. I feel more free and uninhibited around other women than I do with my significant other.

7. I feel unappreciated by my significant other.

8. I feel uncomfortable asking my significant other for help, even when I really need it.

9. I don't feel sexy when I'm with my significant other.

10. The responsibilities I have to carry in my relationship make me feel more like a slave than a husband or boyfriend.

11. I have not discussed my sexual desires and satisfaction with my mate.

12. I have not asked my mate about her sexual desires and level of satisfaction.

13. My mate's family/friends have an undue influence on our relationship.

14. My significant other doesn't know about my painful past.

15. My significant other uses my past to manipulate me.

16. I feel that I have to try to be superman in my relationship.

17. I feel that I can't fulfill my part of the financial relationship.

18. My mate doesn't seem to feel safe and secure with me.

19. There are some things in our relationship that could tear us apart if we don't deal with them.

20. I feel that my mate doesn't understand my inner feelings.

21. My mate knows of my inner feelings but doesn't seem interested in their effect on me.

22. My mate feels threatened anytime I try to improve myself.

RESULTS

Rate your responses on the scale below.

0–4 "true" responses = Connected Lover
5–10 "true" responses = Hidden Lover
11–15 "true" responses = First-Degree Hidden Lover
16 or more "true" responses = Hard-Core Hidden Lover

SO WHAT CAN WE (MEN AND WOMEN) DO ABOUT IT?

First, hidden lovers have to identify themselves as such and they have to want to change—not only for the sake of their relationships, but for themselves. If they want to change for any other reason, it's a change only on the surface. If you love a hidden lover, you have to realize that you can't change him. However, you can play a significant supporting role in his change. Throughout the rest of this book, I'll explore the hidden lover and discuss some real strategies for change and personal transformation. But as you read, remember that discovering these issues and working to change them is a process that doesn't happen overnight.

THE TRANSFORMATIVE EFFECT OF KEEPING A JOURNAL

While reading this book, it will help to keep a journal. I've found writing in a journal to be a great way to release energy and patch the soul when it is wounded. It is a great creative resource as well. What you write—be it details of your personal life, concepts or snippets and stories from your day—is up to you. A journal can be a great way to let off steam or deal with some pent-up energies.

However, as to how journal writing relates to this book, I have some specific suggestions. Writing in a journal is a particularly effective means to delve into feelings. It's a place to have a one-way conversation about anything you like. You can dump feelings, ideas or fears there without ever having to worry about what someone will say. You can rant, rave or just go off if you want to and you never have to worry about having someone else attempt to argue with you about it. For the time you're writing in your journal, it's all about what you're feeling.

I encourage everyone reading this book (man or woman) to start a journal and follow along with the journalizing exercises at the end of each chapter. Your journal doesn't have to be elaborate. But it is best if it is something bound because you'll want to go back and revisit your thoughts days, months, even years later. You can pick up a simple spiral notebook from the grocery store; or if you prefer, fancier journals are available at bookstores, department stores and specialty shops.

Keep your journal in a safe place, even under lock and key if necessary! Since it contains deep feelings and emotions, it isn't to be shared with just anyone. And it certainly shouldn't be left anywhere it could be picked up by someone else. Someone reading your journal is the same as someone eavesdropping on you. The person will likely see things he or she isn't supposed to see, doesn't understand, and therefore will misinterpret. Protect your journal to protect your privacy.

THINGS TO THINK ABOUT

1. Do the questions on the hidden lover quiz remind you of someone you've ever been involved with (or are involved with now)?
2. Do you feel you are play-acting in your relationships with the opposite sex? If so, where did you learn that role? How can you get out of that role and be yourself?
3. What are some things about yourself you may be hiding in relationships?

JOURNAL ENTRY

How well do you think you know your mate? List four things (about him) that you know. On this list, mix simple and complex items. An example of a simple item would be his or her favorite food. An example of a complex item would be knowing the story behind a person or event that significantly changed his or her life.

A LETTER FROM THE HIDDEN LOVER, PART 1

I'm going to be perfectly honest with you as I write these letters, even if it means saying things that may not sound so great. The reason I'm going to be so straightforward is that I need to say these things. I have stuff that I carry around with me that stresses me out sometimes so much that I feel trapped. And if that isn't bad enough, those things often have to do with you, the woman in my life, the woman I want to have a close and intimate relationship with.

But having said that, I have to be honest and say that there's a history behind some of the issues I have which goes beyond my relationship with you. Some of these issues and blocks to intimacy and closeness started a long time ago. You didn't really have anything to do with them. Yet they still affect me today, and therefore us as a couple.

On the other hand, some of the things that tend to stand between us aren't connected to my past and are problems or issues that you and I have. I feel that if you were aware of these things, maybe you could change them, or at least do them less frequently. But we'll get to that in another letter. Right now I just want to keep writing about how I feel. I'm able to write these things to you in a letter better than I think I can say them. I really believe that after I've written these letters and you've read them I'll feel more comfortable about opening up to you. You'll know an entirely different side of me that you didn't know existed. It's funny how we sometimes think we know all there is to know about a person and then suddenly we find out there's a lot more to them than what we knew—and how that changes the way we look at them and feel about them forever. That's the feeling you'll get as you read my letters. You're going to see the man you love in another light.

But don't look for me to change overnight. It's going to take time. Believe it or not, I've been trying to change for a while now. In fact, in my mind at least, I have changed. I can even give you a couple of examples.

Remember how you used to get upset because I didn't seem to enjoy holding hands in public? Well, if you recall, last weekend as we left the movie it was I who initiated our holding hands instead of you. As usual, I felt a little uncomfortable because I'm not into public displays of affection, but instead of drawing my hand away, I just tuned everybody else out.

Also, though you may not know it, I've been doing a lot of thinking lately. Last year when we felt like we were going to call it quits was an important time for me. That was when I realized that my hard exterior was protecting me and helping me feel strong, but it wasn't helping our relationship. It was weird, but when we talked openly about what we had to do to stay together, though I may have acted unemotional, I was all stirred up inside. I actually liked talking to you about all that. Only I don't want to have to come to the point of breaking up again in order to air things out. I want to learn to get feelings and issues out into the open in a way that doesn't hurt.

I guess this is about me learning to be more tuned in to my senses. I don't like to use the term "getting in touch with my feminine side." I prefer to look at myself in the same light as the ancient poet-warriors. They were strong and fierce fighting men, but they appreciated and valued their emotional and aesthetic side. I've learned from that example that if I become a little more sensitive, it will make me feel like a stronger man because then I won't be afraid of what I'm feeling anymore; feelings can then be powerful assets to me in my life. Being afraid of my own feelings has made me do some crazy things before and I don't want to go there anymore. Some guys don't think a man can be masculine and sensitive, but now I know I can be both and that's what being a man really is all about.

Last, the fact that I'm writing these letters is evidence for you that I really want to be a man who is more open and intimate in his relationship. I know that for our love to grow I've got to be more giving of my emotional self, to be more than a provider and a protector. This letter is a step in that direction.

You see, my dear, I do want to be close to you. But it's not easy for me. I'm sure it isn't exactly easy for you to reach out and be close either. But for me as a man, it is a really tough task because reaching out or opening up makes me feel vulnerable and that's a feeling that is at the top of the list of hardest things for men to do. For you, and our relationship, I'm now willing to experience whatever it takes to make me a better man and to therefore improve our relationship.

CHAPTER 2

HOW HIDDEN LOVERS HIDE IN RELATIONSHIPS

The first fact to realize about a hidden lover is that he is a man in a committed relationship—that is, a marriage, a long-term relationship, or even a serious dating relationship. The hidden lover is a man who's made a commitment, at least on the surface. Yet inside, he's still tentative about connecting himself to the woman he loves. In essence, he's hiding within himself while in a relationship, and that invariably leads to problems.

Hidden lovers use three methods to hide within relationships. First, they close themselves off; second, they back away from the relationship, using space and time as a shield; or third, they do a disappearing act. Why would a man say he wants to be in a close and intimate relationship and then close off, back away or even just disappear? It seems illogical, but, every day, hidden lovers do it.

When it comes to the hidden lover disappearing into hiding, there are basically two reasons. First, though he was initially attracted to the idea of having a relationship, he now feels overwhelmed by it (please refer to Chapter 6, How Fear of Losing Freedom Affects the Hidden Lover). Second, he has unresolved issues he's dealing with that were triggered by the relationship (please refer to Chapter 3, His Hidden Pain). Disappearing acts of hidden lovers could range from a guy suddenly becoming aloof during a serious dating relationship, or just outright disappearing, to more complex situations in which men in long-term relationships or marriages become closed off or emotionally inactive.

Following are two examples of hidden lovers in hiding.

A DATING DISAPPEARING ACT

Consider the dating situation of Ron and Marie. Ron was a tall, dark and handsome man who'd played college basketball. Though he was now in his late twenties, Ron still maintained his hourglass shape and strong muscle tone.

Marie was an attractive woman with a svelte body, long beautiful legs and a cheerful attitude. She worked in the same office building as Ron but in a different firm. Every morning she would see Ron in the deli sitting alone drinking coffee and perusing the paper. He didn't look as though he was concentrating very hard and many times she'd thought about boldly going over to talk to him. What do I have to lose, she figured. Marie had been divorced for two years and noticed Ron didn't have a ring on his finger.

Yet for a different reason every day she never made a move on Ron. Then one day, as fate would have it, she was running late. She stopped in to the deli to grab a cappuccino-to-go. Everything was a blur because she had an early meeting to make and not a moment to spare. She paid the cashier, grabbed her coffee, and turned quickly to head out. But as she turned she crashed into a tall, dark and handsome man, spilling coffee all over what was obviously not a cheap suit. As the coffee dripped down to his shiny shoes, she looked into his face. At that moment she was smitten. She almost forgot about the coffee dripping all over him. Ron was even more handsome up close than he was from a distance. He had dimples and innocent eyes.

The incident ended with Marie dabbing Ron's suit with a napkin and Ron using the situation to make a love connection with the attractive thirty-something woman he'd just had the fortune to bump into. Within ten minutes they went from a pedestrian accident, to smiles and giggles, to exchanging phone numbers and setting a lunch date.

Fast-forward three months. Lunch dates, dinners and weekends in the park had become the norm for Ron and Marie. Every morning, they'd try to meet for coffee. Every afternoon, they had lunch together at one of the restaurants in the area. On Fridays, they'd sneak away for a long lunch at a little bistro by the lake. After lunch they'd walk and hold hands, sneaking kisses in the rose garden.

Since they'd met, they were both on cloud nine. Ron loved Marie's soft voice. He loved her conservative but sexy style. Marie couldn't believe that she'd met a guy like Ron. He wasn't just another hard-bodied ex-jock. He could play basketball with the boys but he could also discuss current events and books. He was always showering her with compliments. And she knew he meant them. More than once he'd said he always wanted to find a woman like her and that he wanted to have more than just a dating relationship with her.

Everything couldn't be better, right?

Wrong!

One Monday morning, Ron didn't show up for their usual coffee. That was okay because sometimes one of them got busy and couldn't make it. Marie figured she'd see him at lunch. Lunchtime came. No Ron. She called and left a couple of messages on his voice mail and one at his home number. But by late afternoon he hadn't returned them. Marie didn't hear from Ron all day.

Marie started to worry. Maybe something had happened to Ron. It wasn't like him not to show up for their regular lunch date. It wasn't like him not to call. He was always such a gentleman. Yet in the back of her mind, she couldn't help but wonder if Ron could be trying to give her the brush-off. But she couldn't run with that thought. It just didn't make sense. After three months of constant time with Ron, she felt she at least knew that he was too into her to just suddenly give her the brush-off.

After Ron missed lunch again on Tuesday and still hadn't called, Marie'd had enough. She got up from her desk, told her secretary she'd be back in twenty minutes and went down a few floors to Ron's office. By now the receptionist knew her so well that she waved her on through. Marie went to Ron's office and opened the door; he was sitting at his desk talking on the phone. He waved to her and smiled as though nothing was wrong. When he hung up the phone Marie didn't hesitate to speak.

"Ron, where have you been. I've been worried about you!"

Ron responded slowly. "I've been here. . . I just felt like doing something different today."

"But why didn't you call and tell me that. We could've done something different. And what about yesterday?"

"I didn't call you because I'm not sure what I wanted to say."

"What do you mean?"

"Marie . . . I really care for you. But I've been thinking a lot and I don't know if I'm ready for . . ." Ron hesitated. "I mean . . ." More hesitation. "What I'm trying to say is—"

"What *are* you trying to say, Ron?"

"Well, I guess I'm just not ready to get any more serious than we are. I think we should just keep dating but not get too serious about everything. I do want to keep seeing you, just not every day."

"Why have you been saying that you've been looking for a woman like me all your life and that you wanted to do more than just date? You said you wanted a relationship, Ron! How can we just go backwards all of a sudden?"

Ron paused. "I know I did. But I guess now I just want to be involved, but not too involved."

Marie's face revealed her total shock. Her budding relationship with Ron had disappeared suddenly and for no apparent reason. What Ron was saying didn't even sound logical. Did he even believe what he was saying?

Marie was hurt beyond words. She felt betrayed by Ron. And she felt stupid for falling for him so deeply, only for him to turn out to be just like all the rest. Could she even trust her judgment anymore? Here she was with another grown man who was all hot and heavy in the beginning and suddenly afraid of his own shadow when things started getting intimate. She was really tired of this same old thing with men. "Never mind, Ron. Don't explain. And don't bother to call me anymore."

Marie wanted to cry. But being a respected woman with an executive position in that same building, she would have to hold back the tears until she could get to her office and close the door. She wanted to slam Ron's office door so hard that the pictures would fall off the wall, but she didn't. She wanted to curse him, but she didn't. She simply closed the door to his office, gathered her composure and walked out, making sure to say a cheerful goodbye to the receptionist. She didn't need her personal business all over his place of business. But she would leave a good piece of her mind on his voice mail at home.

Sounds crazy, right? Just when things seem that they could get no better, Ron has withdrawn from the relationship. What happened? Was it something she said or did? Is there someone else? Is Ron getting cold feet? Did he just want sex? Read the following section to understand what was going on in Ron's head.

STAGES OF A DATING DISAPPEARING ACT

Act I: Boy meets girl

In the beginning everything is new and exciting. Everything about the new woman in his life excites a man—her voice, her hair, her shape, the smell of her perfume, etc. Even quirky little things about her appearance or personality are considered cute or unique. He's always thinking about her, replaying her words in his head and remembering her smile.

Act II: Fun and games

In this stage a man is starting to incorporate this exciting new woman into his life. Still beaming from the thrill of being involved with this new woman, he enjoys talking to her as much as possible and he sees her as much as possible. That's the fun part. But the games begin as he starts to feel himself become closer to this woman. Perhaps he is starting to feel more obligated than he would like. Or he could be feeling a deep connection forming that he is uncomfortable with. Or perhaps this relationship is triggering some painful issues from past occurrences in his life. To counteract his feeling of being out of control and swept away by his feelings, he may start subtle games of manipulation in order to gain control of the situation. Or he may try to create distance from her as a means of creating a safety zone. He could also be beginning to see her as a real person with flaws instead of the absolute perfection he imagined her to be. For example, some of the things he thought were cute and quirky may be getting on his nerves now.

Act III: The crossroad

As time passes, he finds himself at a crossroad. He really likes this woman. He may feel that he loves her. Now what? Should he commit himself to a relationship with her? Should he dive into a relationship and take on the related responsibilities, the risk of being hurt, and face the unknown? Or should he hide by remaining on his own, where he feels safe and secure? The irony is that he actually does want to have a relationship but his growing apprehension is so strong that he's thrown into a dilemma. He's left with the decision of either making a commitment or disappearing.

Act IV: The disappearing act

Feeling overwhelmed by the apprehension of having a relationship, he disappears. He may do this in one of several ways. The easiest method is the call screen. Another method is to always have an excuse for being unavailable. The most extreme method is to simply vanish, disappear by cutting all communication and contact.

THREE DATING DISAPPEARING ACTS AND WHAT THEY MAY MEAN

Now that we've looked at the dating disappearing act, let's look at some common reasons for this occurrence. (Of course, this is assuming the couple was dating as seriously as Ron and Marie in the example.) I stress the word "common" because there are so many variables that it would be illogical to attempt to speak in absolutes. Despite interviewing many men and being one myself, I can't state an absolute reason as to why each man in each specific situation does what he does. But here are some common reasons.

1. Wolf Man

We all know this guy. He just wanted a consistent sex partner
for a while. He got it and now he's gone. Thank-you-ma'am
(some don't even say that much). Wolf man will do whatever
is necessary to get a woman into bed. He will lie, wine and
dine her, buy her gifts. . . whatever it takes. But after he's had
as much as he wants, he's gone. Wolf man is different from a
guy who disappears after sex once or a few times because he
lingers around for months. But eventually he runs back into
the woods to stalk more prey.

2. Man in Hot Pursuit

This guy is really a hoot. He goes after a woman hard with
all he's got. He's obsessed. All he can think about is her.
As far as he's concerned, she's the most perfect woman in
the world. He is absolutely convinced that she is the woman
for him. But a funny thing happens when the man in hot
pursuit gets his prize. After the woman he seeks says, "I'm
yours," he hits the brakes hard. After months of trying to
get her to notice him, he suddenly doesn't seem interested in her at the level he once was. This guy may have been
on an ego trip just to see if he could "catch" her. Or he
was only interested in the woman when she was a fantasy of perfection to him. When he got to know her better

she couldn't live up to his fantasy notions and he was disappointed.

3. Mr. Freeze

Like Marie in the example, you're dating a guy who seems perfect for you in every way. You've told all of your friends about him. He's met your parents. You're even starting to dream of a future with him. Suddenly, he starts acting funny. It usually happens as a slow process. Not calling as much. Not being as available. Acting fickle or irritable. Slowly he just withdraws from you. When you confront him about his behavior he thinks you're overreacting, or he blames it on work or some other good excuse. But if his behavior persists, it's probably more than that. Men freeze up for several reasons:

1. He may not feel comfortable advancing to a deeper intimacy (this may or may not have anything to do with the woman he is involved with).
2. He may be having doubts about the woman he's involved with.
3. He may be having doubts about his ability to handle a relationship.
4. He could have a new romantic interest in his life.

Now let's look at the other side of the coin, hidden lovers in marriages and long-term relationships.

HOW HIDDEN LOVERS DISAPPEAR IN MARRIAGES AND LONG-TERM RELATIONSHIPS

The disappearing acts of hidden lovers change after they are married or in long-term relationships. Interestingly, hidden lovers in long-term relationships or marriages often have a disappearing act which doesn't involve leaving the relationship. Instead, it often involves remaining in the relationship in the role of boyfriend or husband while checking out of the relationship emotionally. They do this for the sake of convenience. They don't want to deal with the aftershocks of a traumatic or costly breakup, so they just adopt a coping mentality and disappear within themselves. The following are ways in which hidden lovers disappear from full participation in a relationship while remaining in the relationship.

The emotional shutdown

Often when we think of men doing a disappearing act, we think of it only in terms of them leaving the relationship. But it isn't always that clear a situation; there is another type of disappearing act done by hidden lovers, particularly by men in long-term relationships or marriages who feel the need to hide part of themselves. In this type of disappearing act, the man doesn't walk out of the relationship. Instead he withdraws emotionally while continuing to fulfill his role in the relationship in a perfunctory and obligatory manner.

The problem with the emotional shut-down begins when a man feels that he has an insurmountable problem in his relationship (see list below). This form of disappearance is probably the biggest threat to a marriage or long-term relationship because it can become the root of so many other problems.

Possible reasons for an emotional shut-down:

1. He feels unfulfilled in his life and feels his relationship is part of the reason.
2. There is an ongoing serious dispute with his significant other.
3. He harbors undisclosed anger or resentment toward his significant other.
4. He is experiencing feelings of sexual inadequacy.
5. He is frustrated with his relationship in general.
6. He is having an affair.

Affairs

Though I've mentioned several reasons for an emotional shutdown, probably the most damaging of them all is the extramarital affair. For that reason, I'm going to elaborate further on the factors involved in hidden lovers having affairs.

At first glance, an affair may not seem to be a way of hiding feelings, but in the hidden lover's case that's exactly the case. When a hidden lover has an affair he's not intending to leave his relationship. It's more a situation of his running away from a problem, even though affairs don't solve problems. For hidden lovers, affairs and extramarital trysts aren't simply about having a sexual opportunity or the way a woman caught their eye. When hidden lovers have affairs it's because, for some reason, they are not connecting in their relationship and see the "other" woman as an opportunity to escape and hide from the reality of the problems they don't want to face in their relationship. But how does this happen to a man who says he wants to improve his relationship? Like everything else, the roots of affairs start small and grow into a big problem if left unaddressed. Let's look at how hidden lovers get themselves into extramarital trouble.

Anatomy of an affair

Among the hidden lovers I talked to on this subject, one was very candid and detailed about his affair. I'll call him "Ray." Ray had really thought the situation through and shared his thoughts with me. Correlating this with the experiences of other hidden lovers, I was able to map the anatomy of an affair. Basically, it happens in five stages:

1. Unmet need—an emotional or sexual desire going unaddressed in his marriage. This could be the fault

of one or both of the people in the marriage.

2. Willingness/desire—an openness on his part to have this desire met by another woman.
3. Opportunity—meeting a woman who is willing to fill his need/desire.
4. Relationship—having a strong and intimate emotional interdependence with a woman other than his wife. (Sometimes this step is skipped and men go straight to step 5.)
5. Infidelity—having a brief or long-term sexual relationship outside his marriage.

Here's a fictional example, a composite derived from several different men. It illustrates how these factors come together.

Ray wasn't looking for a sexual relationship. But he was frustrated with his life and career. He'd been married for close to ten years and had two kids. He was a good man who worked hard to provide for his family. But for a couple of years he had been harboring a great deal of guilt about the fact that his wife and kids wanted a bigger, more expensive home in a better neighborhood. This was made worse by the fact that all of his friends had moved up the corporate ladder as he continued to be passed over for promotion. Though his wife worked full-time as well, he felt that he, as the man of the house, should've been able to earn the additional income necessary to move his family up a notch on the socioeconomic ladder. Often his wife and kids would go dream home browsing on Sunday afternoons and would come home with hopeful faces and hand him brochures. Or worse, they'd go visit friends who'd moved up to nicer homes in upscale neighborhoods and return with stories about their beautiful homes. Being a hidden lover, Ray never shared with his wife and kids how unappreciated and inadequate all of that made him feel. Since he never shared his feelings of inadequacy with anyone, he imploded, suffering a great loss of self-esteem and often becoming depressed.

It was his low self-esteem and feelings of being unappreciated that opened the door to an affair with his co-worker Juanita. It all started one day when he peeked into her office to say good-morning. She was sitting at her desk looking sullen. Normally she was perky, so he asked her what was wrong. They started talking and she told him that she and her husband had been arguing a lot lately about any and every thing. Ray shared with her the fact that he was feeling bad that he wasn't able to support his family the way he wanted. They ended up closing the door to her office and spending about an hour talking and sharing. Ray liked talking to Juanita; she'd always been his favorite person in the office. But that was the first time they ever talked so intimately with each other about their lives.

Over the next few weeks, Ray and Juanita continued to talk privately and gave each other advice and encouragement. Ray came to work each morning looking forward to those talks as the highlight of his day. Often, he thought, "I wish my wife were more like Juanita; she totally understands that we don't need to buy an expensive new home." But all of their talks didn't help either of their lives at home. Juanita's marriage was getting worse and Ray's family was still pressuring him to buy a new home. One afternoon when they were supposed to have lunch together they didn't make it out of the parking garage because as soon as Juanita got into the car, she broke into tears. Ray spent the entire lunch hour consoling her. It was the first time they'd ever hugged.

Ray felt something during that hug. He was falling for Juanita and he could see in Juanita's eyes that she was falling for him too. His feelings for her were strong. Ray wondered how Juanita's husband could have such a great wife and not know it. He was even growing jealous of her husband. In his mind he often flirted with thoughts of having a wild secret affair with her, but he fought the feelings, believing they'd pass.

But all of that changed the Friday afternoon they first kissed. Ray and Juanita had developed a habit of parking next to each other in the garage so they could talk as they left the office for the day. Every day, they'd exchange a big hug before getting into their cars. They had become very close. Emotionally, Ray felt closer to Juanita than his wife. On that Friday both of them were lingering, not wanting to say goodbye. It was cold so they sat inside Ray's car talking and laughing. They sat there so long that all of the other cars had left the garage. Suddenly, they stared at each other through an awkward pause in the laughter. They kissed. It was a culmination of all the sexual tension that had been building since they had begun their affair of the heart. For fifteen minutes, they were like two high school kids making out in the car.

Before leaving, they constructed a plan for a rendezvous. Monday, Juanita would call in sick and then go check into a motel. Then she would call Ray at work and give him the room number. They had sex all afternoon. Ray didn't get back to work until 4:30. After that, they met several other times at motels. Each time, they worked together to construct schemes that covered their tracks flawlessly.

But after a couple of months of sneaking around, everything dissolved. As they were lying in bed at a motel during an extended Friday lunch break, Juanita began to cry. She confessed her guilt and said that even though her husband was being a jerk, she wanted to work it out with him or call it quits the right way. She said she didn't want to sneak around and lie to him, or to herself, or do anything that would hurt her kids. Juanita said the affair wasn't helping, only making her life more confusing. Ray didn't fight it; she was right. He felt the same way too. With that, they cut it off without another word. No long good-byes, no closure. Later, Juanita resigned her position at the company. Ray never heard from her after that.

After Ray's delusion of escaping his problems with an affair had dissipated, he was left not only with his original problems, but also with the guilt of having had an affair. Ray could've possibly solved his problem by sharing with his wife how painful it was to him that he couldn't provide a higher quality of living for the family. Then he and his wife could've sat down with the kids and explained economic realities to them, perhaps even helping them appreciate what they already had. But as a hidden lover, he feared telling them his innermost feelings, these feelings that made him feel most vulnerable.

The walkout

The last and most critical form of disappearing act in a relationship is the walkout. When a man feels he just can't take it anymore and hasn't the tools to deal with expressing his feelings, he may walk out. As I stated previously, this isn't as likely because hidden lovers have so much invested in their relationships. Moreover, this isn't likely for most hidden lovers because they want to work on their relationships. But everyone has heard the story of a friend or friend of a friend whose spouse simply turned to them one day after years of marriage or a long committed relationship and said they wanted out, or simply left. This type of situation ties together closely with the emotional shut-down. Usually a person wouldn't leave without some clues as to how he was dissatisfied with the relationship. When men are in the emotional shut-down mode, they continue an act for as long as they can. Then some eventually tire of the act and put an end to it by walking out.

DON'T FORGET TO LOOK AT YOUR ROLE IN THE SITUATION

When examining how hidden lovers disappear whether it is a shut-down or outright walkout, it's important for their mates to look at what role they may be playing in the situation although they may not even realize it. Maybe you didn't pay attention. Maybe you didn't heed the red flags. Was he a silver-tongued devil who charmed you so well that you decided to throw caution to the wind? Is he so smooth that he just outright fooled you, or did you hear what you wanted to hear and see what you wanted to see when it came to this Romeo?

I know lots of women are saying, "I've been there. I know about men and their disappearing acts." But over and over, men talk about how so many women see and hear what they want to instead of listening to what men are telling them.

For example, one fellow told me a story of how he was accused of leaving a woman at the altar. His side of the story is that she was pushing the entire marriage on him from the beginning. He says while he had discussed marriage with her as something he would eventually like to do, he hadn't proposed to her or committed to the idea. Yet, his girlfriend made herself a fiancée and went forward with wedding plans believing that he would eventually come around. She put a deposit down at a church and was starting to negotiate with caterers and florists. She was even setting the date—a date that her man was not prepared to make! As the date approached she realized his cold feet weren't going to warm up and she canceled the reservations and plans. They broke up (but have continued seeing each other on and off—that's another story altogether).

She accused her boyfriend of standing her up, but did he? Or did she just get an idea and run with it? I mentioned this story because it happens, in varying degrees, a lot in the relationship world—whether it's a marriage or just a misunderstanding about a dating relationship. Some women want a particular man so much that they start imagining things that aren't there. It's very important to be on level ground before you look at the guy and say he's wrong. It's true that far too many men are guilty of disappearing acts, but sometimes they were saying, or at least showing you, where they were going all along.

THINGS TO THINK ABOUT

1. In this chapter, the stages of a disappearing act were discussed. At which stage could more honest communication help avoid a disappearing act?
2. How is it possible for one partner to be seemingly satisfied with a relationship while the other views it as a bad relationship?
3. What can a woman do to find closure when a man walks out on her without giving a reason or saying good-bye?

JOURNAL ENTRY

Think of a disappearing act, shut-down or walkout you've been involved in. Were you the person who left or did he leave you? Perhaps you've had experiences on both sides of the situation. Write a fictional account of what you think the other person might have been feeling when they shut down, walked out or disappeared. Or write what you were feeling when you shut down, walked out or disappeared.

A LETTER FROM THE HIDDEN LOVER, PART 2

I guess you wonder how this entire hidden lover issue could even exist for me in our relationship. You probably wonder how and where I could do all of that hiding. Well, you have to remember that the hiding is done on the inside and it is only evident in my actions. But then sometimes my actions don't reveal what I'm feeling because I'm so good at hiding things I don't want to discuss or deal with.

I remember when I was dating, hiding in a relationship was so much easier. When I was dating different women, I never really had to get particularly close to any of them if I didn't want to. The whole idea of dating was exploring other people, not necessarily bonding with all of them. So for me, as a hidden lover, dating was a very safe place for me to stay comfortably neutral. If I felt things were getting more intimate, I could go as far as I wanted to. Since I wasn't actually committed to the woman I was dating and she wasn't around me all the time, I could still conceal anything I wanted to conceal from her. In essence, I could control how close we became.

Of course, as someone got to know me better, that became more difficult. There were times when I had to decide if I wanted to become intimately connected with some women because we were spending so much time together that they were able to read me. That was okay if I felt a closeness. But for those I didn't feel close to, it was time to disconnect. That's what was convenient about dating. If something didn't click, it was easy to just get out of it. All it took was a phone call or the infamous "it isn't working out" conversation.

But now as a man who has committed myself, I have a different issue altogether. I can't just hide from you when something isn't going the way I want, because a marriage is no place to hide my feelings. I can't just drop you off at your place and then drive away from issues and situations, because we live together. If something's bothering me about us, or even a personal matter, I can't just grin and bear it until the end of a date and then we go our separate ways. What affects me also affects you, since our lives are now intermingled.

But that still doesn't mean that I disclose the things to you I think you might need to know in order to help me when I need help or make us stronger as a couple when we are struggling with an issue together. That's because I just don't always feel comfortable or safe doing that (I'll tell you more about that in another letter). Instead of hiding my feelings when I have something difficult to share or discuss, I have basically two choices: shut down or go off the deep end and do something crazy like have an affair.

So how have I dealt with these situations? Which form of hiding have I used? You can relax; I haven't had any affairs. I feel that would be crazy because it would add to any problems that I already had by complicating my life, not to mention hurting you. What I've done in the past is to just shut down and shut you out, hide within myself. I've done it more times than I can remember. I know you may not understand, but sometimes it is just too hard or too inconvenient to face something so I just swallow it and that's what creates hidden feelings, fears and pains inside me.

CHAPTER 3

HIS HIDDEN PAIN

This is a critical issue in understanding the hidden lover's behavior. Some men have hidden the deep pain from relationships inside themselves and have never been able to resolve it. Some people say, "Why don't they get help?" There are two answers to that question. First, many men don't feel comfortable saying they are powerless to handle a problem, relationship or otherwise. Second, men have generally been slow to embrace the idea of getting help through therapy. One major fear of men about therapy is that they could be seen as unfit to perform their jobs. They fear possible repercussions in their career or income if it somehow became known they were seeking therapy. At the very least, they fear being seen as weak or even ridiculed if their reasons for seeking therapy were known. So instead of getting help, many men suffer in silence as various issues from their past eat away inside them.

The emotional pain some men have stored up from relationships can come from any of a number of sources. Interestingly, those sources of relationship pain don't necessarily have to be from romantic relationships. For lots of men, their problems in relationships come from their childhood. The issues men have shared with me through interviews and conversations are discussed in this chapter.

EXAMPLES OF POOR RELATIONSHIPS

Example of a poor relationship between his parents

Let's start at the beginning. Some guys had such awful examples of relationships from their parents that they have difficulty today having relationships as adults. The behavior they saw modeled in relationships could have been fathers and mothers who battled verbally. Or perhaps there was physical abuse of the mother by the father, or vice versa. Perhaps even the children were abused. For men who grew up in such an environment, it can become difficult to even imagine a loving healthy relationship.

There are a lot of men who don't have a healthy relationship with their fathers because their fathers have never been present in their lives. They may have fathers who have come in and out of their lives, or the type of father who was physically present but so distant that he never played the role of a "daddy." Last, there are fathers who disappeared into thin air after a divorce. All of these men not only leave scars in the hearts of their children; they also leave a legacy of pain that can haunt the relationships of their children if these issues are never resolved.

Of course, there are also mothers who have been poor models for intimate behavior. For example, some have brought too many dates around their young children, thus giving them mixed signals about the longevity of relationships. Some have ignored or even neglected their children in order to spend time gaining the favor of a man or pursuing a relationship. Then there are mothers who remain with men who are not good for them or the children, allowing the children to view a poor example of a relationship. Also there's the mother who is always desperately searching for a man in her life. Just as with poor fathering examples, these women model behaviors that can have lasting negative effects on how men view intimacy and relationships.

Finally, another poor example of relationships in the home exists where the father and the mother live in active contempt of one another. Inevitably the children pick up negative ideas about relationships from them. Although the parents in this situation may not be throwing chairs at each other, they constantly make degrading and insulting comments about each other to the children. Needless to say, this behavior works its way into the views of relationships held by the children.

Being involved in a divorce

Some of the most bitter men I've ever met are those who are divorced. If I'd listened to any of them, I would've never gotten married. Here is some of the advice I've collected from them over the years:

> "Whatever you do, don't ever get married."
> "A woman will smile in your face and cheat on you as soon as you walk out the door."
> "Marry a woman who has more to lose than you if there's a divorce."
> "Forget about love and all that stuff. Make your marriage a strictly business arrangement."

Why are these men so bitter? They're bitter because they took a chance on love and it didn't work out for them. The pain is multiplied exponentially if the man really committed himself to the relationship and feels he wasn't appreciated. Or worse, he was cheated on. Sure, women deal with this all the time and get over it. But for men to come out of the shell and take a chance requires what we feel is a huge risk because we've been conditioned to keep ourselves protected and closed off. Therefore, when we sincerely open up and get hurt, it's devastating. I'm not saying women are always less devastated, but, generally speaking, most women tend to process their emotions better than men. On the other hand, men don't typically confront their emotional pain. Instead, they deny it and put on a mask of machismo. The result is that a man may say he's recovered from a divorce while really hiding the pain—possibly for years or even the rest of his life if he never seeks to heal himself.

Torn relationships

It doesn't always take a nasty divorce to scar a man when it comes to relationships. Like divorces, torn relationships leave deep wounds. Take Ed, for example:

Ed says he has problems trusting women in a relationship. He was in a year-long relationship with a woman who became pregnant. She told him the baby was his and she hadn't been with anyone since dating him exclusively. He assumed the child was his and began working overtime at his job to help with the expenses of the pregnancy. He also made plans to leave the job he loved to take a position he didn't like because he needed better pay and benefits. When the baby was born he recalls having some doubts whether it was his child. He recalls not ever feeling that she was totally honest with him during their year together. However, though he was sometimes suspicious, he never had any hard evidence of her cheating on him.

But as a precaution he followed his hunch and asked her if she and the baby would take a simple DNA test. His girlfriend was insulted and she cried and fussed with him for months, but finally agreed. The test results bore out his hunch: the baby wasn't his. He had been deceived. He was crushed and it took him years to call another woman his girlfriend. Even then, it took a long time for him to trust the current woman in his life.

Observing bad relationships of friends

Some men don't want to get into relationships because of what they've seen their friends going through in relationships. More specifically, several specific phases that they've seen their friends go through.

The first is *disappearing*. Many guys who get into relationships seem to drop off the planet. Suddenly, they don't see their old buddies much anymore. They rarely call. For example, let's say a guy used to meet his friends for a basketball game every Saturday morning followed by lunch. After he started a new relationship, he showed up only a couple of times every month and then rushed off after the game, never having time to socialize or go to lunch with the guys anymore. It's quite possible that this guy may have just been so smitten by his newfound love that he didn't want to hang out with the guys as much as he used to. However, from the standpoint of those on the outside looking in, this is an example of a woman taking a man hostage, a denial of his freedom.

The second phase men observe other men going through is *the roller-coaster* effect it has on their friend's emotions. Though they may not see him as much after he gets into a relationship, he does surface from time to time. When he does, he is either high as a kite on love, or he's down in the dumps. After his friends see this cycle enough, they wonder why the guy is in the relationship at all.

The third observance is the *crash-and-burn*. This is the point at which the relationship ends and the guy returns to his buddies. He's wounded, angry and bitter so he returns to headquarters with reports of women and relationships as the enemy. For the other guys, many of whom are already on their way to being hidden lovers due to their own deep-seated fears about relationships, this only reinforces what they were already afraid of and causes them to redouble their avoidance of relationships and true intimacy.

An alternative to the crash-and-burn is the *final withdrawal*. This is when the relationship becomes so all-encompassing that a guy's life begins to orbit around it. From the outside, it appears he has no life other than his relationship. At this point, his friends can write him off. Other than receiving a wedding invitation, they won't be hearing from this guy anymore. Sure, they'll talk in passing and promise to get together, but it probably won't happen. Basically, they can write him off. I've always thought this was a sad part of male friendships. Ever since high school, I remember seeing this pattern. I've been guilty of it myself. We seem to act as though we can have only one major source of emotional support in our lives—a serious relationship or the guys. On the other hand, women tend to have entire systems of emotional support. This is something we need to emulate. If men weren't so extreme about their behavior changes when in a relationship, lots of other men wouldn't see relationships as such a frightening mystery.

Last, there's the *ball-and-chain*. When men observe their friends go into marriages, for example, and suddenly become laden down with a myriad of new bills, responsibilities and children, some of them are scared out of their wits. This usually isn't helped much when the guy who has all of these responsibilities complains about it to his friends.

I remember having a conversation with one of my students before a class. He was a young man in his early twenties who'd been working all day, and he looked so tired that I didn't know how he was going to stay awake during the class. He told me he was tired because he'd worked twelve hours that day. Then he said he had to go pick up the baby from his sister-in-law's house across the city after class. His face was sincere when he spoke these words. "I wish I'd never gotten married. I had a really easy life and now I've messed all of that up."

For more on how the ball-and-chain feeling affects hidden lovers, read Chapter 6, How Fear of Losing Freedom Affects a Hidden Lover.

HIDDEN SEXUAL ABUSE

While being interviewed for this book, several men divulged that they had been sexually abused as children. This is an important issue as it directly affects a man's perception of a relationship as well as how he will conduct himself within one. According to Prevent Child Abuse America, approximately one in six boys is sexually abused before age sixteen.

An area that causes immense pain for some men is the lingering pain of having been sexually abused. Often, sexual abuse brings images of women and little girls to mind. But abuse happens to boys (and men) as well. In fact, one of the things that makes it so difficult for men to deal with is that our society often thinks of women and girls as the only victims of sexual abuse. Therefore, men who have been abused as boys (or adults) may carry around the pain and not receive help because they are embarrassed, feeling isolated or not properly identified by mental health professionals.

We need to take the issue of sexual abuse of men and boys as seriously as we do that of girls and women. To not do so is to be irresponsible as a society. If you're a man who has been sexually abused as a child, seek help. There are resources in the back of this book to help you.

HOW MEN TYPICALLY DEAL WITH EMOTIONAL PAIN

It never ceases to amaze me how women don't mind talking and sharing even the most intimate details of their lives with a perfect stranger. Men hardly ever do that with friends, much less anyone else. Opening up isn't something most men have the tools to do (until they create them through practice). Instead, we just swallow the pain.

What do men do with all of this pain that they've swallowed? It depends on the man. Men who aren't hidden lovers have friends, family or professionals to help them sort through pain. But hidden lovers are closed off; they don't have constructive ways to vent pent-up feelings and emotions. Therefore when they have a problem, they're at risk of defaulting to smoking it out, punching it out, drowning it in alcohol, trying to sedate it with drugs or attempting to lose it between the sheets with women.

In other words, part of dealing with pain for many men is to not deal with the pain, but to mask it, hide it or avoid it. But that brings no solutions, only more pain. What many men need to do is to take the first step toward healing their pain. That first step is an admission of their pain, fears and vulnerabilities. Before saying anything to anyone else about his pain, a man needs to admit his feelings to himself and get some perspective on it. Then he can move on to sharing it with others who can help him deal with the issues he is facing.

FIVE PAINFUL THINGS MEN WON'T ADMIT TO WOMEN

In this chapter, I've presented some issues regarding the emotional pain men hide that impacts their relationships. In this section, I want to take the matter a step further to reveal some of the feelings women often don't know men are experiencing. Here are some things many men would like to tell women, but feel they can't.

I'm afraid.

Men typically don't feel that expressing fear is something they can do without ridicule or losing the respect or admiration of their significant other. Men want to appear powerful and fearless. Of course, this is in contradiction to human nature, because all people experience fear. It's natural. However, many men see admitting fear as something that will lower their value in the eyes of their significant other because they feel their value is based on their strength.

I feel inadequate.

When a man feels that he can't meet the needs of his significant other or family, he can start to feel inadequate. But instead of expressing this to a woman, most men will hide it because admitting a feeling of inadequacy would be taken by many men as an indictment of their manhood. They would feel they weren't useful. When a man tries to hide feelings of inadequacy, it doesn't work for long because the feeling of being useful is so important to most men that without it they would hardly be able to sustain a successful relationship.

I feel unimportant to you.

Similar to feeling inadequate is the feeling of being unimportant. If a man feels unimportant, he basically feels he has no value to a woman. This is probably because one of the main ways men feel valued is through doing something for their mate. I'm not at all suggesting that feeling valued only for what we can do is the ideal way to express ourselves, but it is a fact of life for many men of today.

I'm afraid you'll leave me.

Many men are haunted by the constant fear that their wife or girlfriend is going to leave them. For some men it is a random feeling. However, others can be obsessive about it. Mind you, this fear isn't limited to men who aren't wealthy or regarded as highly attractive. Rather, it springs from personal insecurities and that feeling knows no boundaries.

I'm afraid you've had better sex with someone else.

Some guys worry that their significant other has been with a more experienced or more exciting lover than they are. I don't want to make this fear worse, but the fact of the matter is that they could be right, but that's a possibility they'll have to live with. Instead of looking at sex as a score sheet, let's change the focus. Ultimately, what I recommend to these guys is that they chill out. Sex starts in the head, not in the bed. If she really loves you, that's what makes the sex good. If the love and intimacy are there, the sex is better with you in the present than with a memory.

THINGS TO THINK ABOUT

1. What hidden pain do you think is in your man's past?
2. Do you ever feel that your man has secret issues that are affecting your relationship with him?
3. Have you shared any of your hidden pain with your man?

JOURNAL EXERCISE

Think of a relationship in which a man caused you a great degree of emotional pain. Write him a letter telling him how he made you feel and how that has affected your life. (Use your own discretion as to whether to send the letter or not.) Then, turn the tables and try to write about what may have happened in his life that could have caused him to treat you so badly.

A LETTER FROM THE HIDDEN LOVER, PART 3

I haven't had the best examples of relationships in my life, and I'm sure that has impacted how I have viewed every relationship I've ever had with a woman in a profound way. You always wondered why I seem distrustful of relationships or even afraid when things seem to go wrong. I think it has to do with what I saw as a kid.

When I was a kid my dad was a stranger to me. I hardly ever saw him because he wasn't much more in my life than a sperm donor. He left my mom high and dry when I was three and my brother was five. Then all through my life I hoped and prayed that he would come back. You know, I had those childhood fantasies that my daddy would come home and whisk us all away to a big mansion somewhere. For a long time, even my mom seemed to hope they'd get back together. She'd be extra beautiful when my dad came by, but he didn't seem interested in her for anything but sex. I know he slept over a few times over the years but that was about it. They never got back together. When we were younger, he'd call on birthdays and some holidays. But over the years we heard less and less from him and soon nothing at all. He sort of just slipped away.

He left my mom in a tough jam supporting two boys on a government clerical worker's income. She dropped out of

night school and never finished her degree because she had
to find a second job to support us. I still feel guilty about that.

Finally one day she did file for child support and had his
sorry ass hauled into court. They garnisheed his check and
that helped us out a lot. Still, more than the money, I wanted
my dad. But after that he never contacted us again. He remar-
ried and I hear had another kid. So that was the view of man
and wife that I had. It really sucks.

Then there's my mom. She was a beautiful young woman
who didn't have any problem meeting men after my father
split. Lots of guys wanted to date my mom. They even wanted to marry her. But it took my mom a few years to date seriously because my dad had left her so burned out on men.

Mom never carried on with men in front of us. But I do
remember walking in on her and a guy making out on the
couch once when she thought my brother and I were out playing. I also remember seeing a naked man walking around in
her bedroom early one Saturday morning. She was asleep and
he was going to the bathroom. He didn't seem to care that the
door was open because he didn't even put on his underwear.
And I also remember that it seemed every week we were
meeting a new guy and she was all happy about him and talking on the phone to her girlfriends, then suddenly we wouldn't
hear about him and a new guy would be knocking on the door.

Eventually she married this schoolteacher. But that only
lasted a year. He wasn't a bad stepfather. But he wasn't a good
one either. He rarely paid attention to us at all. We moved

into his house but that wasn't for long. They were always arguing and the next thing I knew we were back in a one-bedroom apartment and in our old school again. I don't think she loved the guy, I just think Mom was tired of carrying all the weight of life on her own.

So as you can see, my initial examples of relationships weren't very strong ones. If I judged all of my relationships by what I'd seen growing up, I wouldn't even believe in marriage or relationships. I had a dad who never showed up in my life and a mom who was looking for love in all the wrong places. My memories are just of people having a haphazard hit-and-miss approach to love. That's just something I wanted you to know.

HOW TRYING TO BE SUPERMAN CREATES A HIDDEN LOVER

The pressure to be superman—all men feel it and virtually all of us attempt to meet the challenge in some form or fashion. But when it comes to hidden lovers, this is another critical issue affecting their relationships because attempting to be superman invariably creates feelings of stress, resentment or even insecurity in men.

Hidden lovers know that they aren't supermen and they'd rather not keep trying to play that role. Truth be told, if they could juggle one fewer ball in the air without it sacrificing the security of their relationships and/or families, they would. But as men, they feel it is their responsibility to play the role of superman in order to be considered "real men." Therefore, even when they've tired of this role, they hold in their true feelings about it.

WHAT'S BEHIND THE DRIVE TO BE SUPERMAN?

Men are not superhuman. But we often think that is what's expected of us. For example, we generally don't like to ask for help and we find it difficult to release things by saying, "I've had enough." Or "I can't handle this."

Many men are particularly afraid of admitting fear, vulnerability or defeat in front of their wife or girlfriend. Behind this fear is the belief that such an admission by a man would lower his woman's opinion of him. We're afraid we'll be called cowardly or wimpy if we can't rise to meet every challenge. True enough, it is important for men to know when to suck it up and get back in there for another round. Part of being a man involves developing the resilience it takes to avoid allowing life's challenges to overcome you. As I always emphasize, there's nothing wrong with a man being a man and exemplifying good strong masculine traits.

But there are also other times when a man needs to know how to back off, retreat or relax. I'm reminded of Oliver Stone's film about the world of pro football, *Any Given Sunday*. There's a scene in which the dangerously injured star quarterback struggles to tell his wife that he's sustained an injury that could not only end his career, but could leave him paralyzed if he were injured again. This was a good example of a man knowing when to back off the superman role. Rather than endanger his health and thus his family's income, he was willing to call it quits. However, there's a twist in this scene. Rather than his wife embracing him and being happy that he made the decision to quit, her response was what every man who shares his vulnerabilities with a woman fears. His wife flew into a rage and basically called him a coward, all culminating with a humiliating slap across his face. Next thing you know, he was back on the field risking a paralyzing injury because he felt the cost of being viewed as a coward by his wife was greater than risking a catastrophic injury.

In a scene from my own life, I think of a basketball game I had with one of the teenagers in my neighborhood. He saw me out shooting baskets in my driveway and asked if I wanted to play a quick game. He was a tall and strong kid who I knew played for the local high school team, so I knew it would probably be a tough match for a guy twice his age whose best sport wasn't basketball anyway. But I wanted to play him because I wanted to be superman. I wasn't going to back down from a challenge, albeit a friendly one. I wanted to feel that there was no challenge I couldn't rise to. We sweated and pounded our way through a game of twenty-one and I hung in there with him. I even managed to sink the last basket to win the game. He congratulated me with a grip and went on his way. I won. And, boy, did I need to. Beating a kid half my age made me feel I still had it. For him it may have just been a quick game. But for me it was the equivalent to the NBA Championship. For a moment, I leaned against the car catching my breath. Suddenly, I was dog-tired and had to go in the house. I work out and swim regularly so I couldn't believe how tired I was. Then it hit me. I wasn't superman. And I sure wasn't seventeen anymore either!

It should also be noted that though the superman tendency is often shown through physical activities, it manifests itself in other ways too. For example, some men use their work as a way to prove they're superman. They work excessively. They routinely volunteer for difficult projects and assignments. Or they are obsessed with some master plan to conquer all of their competition. Again, it's important to note here that I'm drawing a fine line between healthy masculinity and self-destructive hyper masculinity. It's normal for men to be competitive, industrious and to want to lead, but that becomes problematic when it goes beyond a healthy desire and becomes an impossible-to-fulfill superman role.

REASONS HIDDEN LOVERS TRY TO BE SUPERMEN

There are three specific kinds of hidden lovers who feel compelled to be supermen.

The winner-take-all superman

The first and most obvious reason hidden lovers strive to be superman is the American tradition. An old adage says, "He who has the gold, rules." The man who conquers gets all the spoils. He gets the fancy cars, the big houses, the beautiful women, the fame and glory. In terms of relationships, this has major significance in the romantic market. The romantic market is strongly influenced by a type of financial survival of the fittest in which the most economically strong men get the best picks among women. This is because sadly, in our society, men who make lots of money are often considered desirable for that fact alone. Case in point is the rise to power of the computer nerd. Remember when computer nerds used to get pushed around in the hallway by all the football players? Remember those guys, skinny and pimple-faced with their big eyeglasses and pocket protectors? Well, today those guys have become the captains of the high-tech revolution, making millions, even billions. Now they're at the top of the financial pecking order; therefore they are among the most desirable. That's the position the winner-take-all superman wants to be in. He wants to be the alpha male. He sees the first position as the most important thing in life because it will bring him all the other things he desires.

The noble superman

The noble superman is the hidden lover who wants to be a hero. He is a latter-day Prince Charming searching for a damsel in distress to rescue. This man wants to find a woman and completely take care of her. He wants to serenade her and sweep her off her feet. Next in his fantasy of being everything to the woman, he wants to pay all of her bills and leave her with not a care or worry in the world. He believes women shouldn't have to work. He believes women should be placed upon a pedestal and admired. Although he may sound like a good find to some women, they should consider the flip side. What happens if the woman this man practically lives to please has a change of heart? What if she tires of sitting home and being lavished upon? If she decides she wants to do something significant with her own mind, the noble superman will start to feel threatened. He feels his importance is due to the fact that he can provide for her. It's a source of pride to him. If she isn't dependent upon him he will have a problem because he wants to be the provider for all of her needs. A woman should think carefully about this type of man because he could be a controlling type, even potentially abusive.

Superman by birthright

This is a hidden lover superman who is compelled by his culture to fit the mold of superhuman. Some cultures emphasize the role of men as being the sole breadwinner, decision maker, disciplinarian, counselor and any and every other role that is of any leadership importance to a couple, family or society. In such scenarios, the man has this role thrust upon him whether he desires it or not. In this role he is solely accountable for the success or failure of the household; he's even solely accountable for the conduct of his wife and children. When we add to this the fact that some cultures also relegate women to a subservient and passive role, we have the formula for a man who will spend his life yoked with the burden of trying to be superman.

HOW PLAYING SUPERMAN AFFECTS A HIDDEN LOVER'S RELATIONSHIP

When a hidden lover attempts to play superman in a relationship, the relationship ultimately becomes just another source of stress and pressure for him, another performance and test for him to prove himself by. For example, let's look at the relationship of a superman. We'll call him Zack. Zack is recently engaged to a woman he has been dutifully and faithfully dating for two years. Every day he calls her at least three times. The first time is a morning check to make sure she's had a good night. The second call is at lunchtime to check on her day. The last call is before she leaves work so he will know her plans and be able to check on her in case something goes wrong. Zack tries to meet his fiancée for lunch as much as possible, although this is difficult because he's a computer technician roving all over the Dallas area on calls all day. However, some days Zack will drive for half his lunch break to see his fiancée for only ten minutes. He spends a chunk of his paycheck wining and dining her and buying her expensive gifts. He pays her cell phone bill and helps pay for her car. With what's left, he pays his rent and for frequent repairs on his aging van. His dutiful actions also extend into the realm of emotions. When Zack's fiancée is upset, he's upset too. When she is feeling down, he can't rest until she's happy. He also takes care of her when she's sick. More than once, he's missed work trying to run errands for her when she had something as simple as a cold. Zack feels it is his duty to provide for all of her needs.

Although Zack is what many women would call a real sweetheart, we should consider a few questions about him:

Can Zack continue to cater to every whim of his mate?

Could some of Zack's strong motivation to be the perfect mate be indications of some issues that could surface later?

What does Zack expect in return for his dutiful service?

NOTE: I want to add an important distinction here between superman and a man who is just doing what needs to be done. This is not to say that a man shouldn't step up to the plate and take care of his loved ones. At times in life for some reason or another, one person does have to care completely for others in a number of ways. The distinction here is that superman wants to take care of everyone, even when they are capable of contributing. Superman wants to be a hero, even when it is wearing him out in the process. He is not the same as a man who is just stepping up to the plate to do what needs to be done.

UNREAL EXPECTATIONS

The superman role is unrealistic, whether it's a belief of the man, the woman, or both of them. Hidden lovers who play superman are bogged down by unrealistic expectations that burden them emotionally. Yet they still feel compelled to pursue fantasies instead of realities of life in relationships. But here's a news flash: a relationship is about as real as you can get in life. So why does the hidden lover continue to attempt to make everything like a fantasy? Often he finds that by releasing the notion of a fantasy relationship with him playing the role of superman, he can actually become more intimately connected to his wife/girlfriend. Following is an interesting and peculiar example of a hidden lover who relinquished his role of superman and thus rediscovered his relationship.

I met Phil during a trip to Maryland last spring as I was on my way to lecture at a university. The drive from the airport to the university was approximately an hour, so the school had dispatched him to meet me at the airport. When I disembarked the plane Phil was there holding a sign with my name on it. He was a cherubic middle-aged fellow with a thick moustache. Immediately we clicked and began to have an interesting conversation. During our talk he said he was divorced, yet he said he'd never felt closer to his ex-wife. Curious, I asked him why. Phil said he now felt closer to his ex-wife because the divorce removed the expectations and pressures that were on him. He said that as her husband, he felt compelled to provide things for her that were beyond his financial capabilities. As a result, he worked two jobs and never had much time to spend with her or to take care of himself. Their relationship became strained and distant. He also gained weight and became depressed.

Phil said they mutually agreed to divorce about a year and a half ago. After the divorce he quit his second job. Relieved that the stress level in his life had dropped, his life began to change for the better. He had time to relax and pursue his hobbies again. He also started walking a couple of miles every day and losing weight. Not long after that he and his ex-wife began to see each other again. "Our relationship now is better than it was when we were married," he said. Phil attributed the new closeness to his ex-wife to his not feeling shackled by all the pressure he'd previously felt. As a result, he was more free and expressive with her than he'd ever been. He even said a possible reconciliation was in the works.

What's up with that? Strange, but I've heard other guys say that about ex-wives and ex-girlfriends. I too experienced that back in my bachelor days. It seems that somewhere, both the man and woman get caught in a set of rigid expectations and rules. The next thing you know you're starring in the roles of girlfriend-boyfriend or husband-wife instead of enjoying what brought you together in the first place. Then after you break up and the pressures of the roles are gone, you are able to rediscover each other. Now, if we could just learn to do that within the relationship, we'd solve the problem of unrealistic expectations altogether!

THINGS HIDDEN LOVER SUPERMAN TYPES FEEL (BUT WOULD NEVER SAY)

Hopefully, Phil's story will alert some men and women to how superman tendencies can slowly sabotage a marriage or relationship. I also want to offer a listing of a few things hidden lovers have said about the pressures they feel in the role of superman—burdens many hidden lovers carry in silence for fear that complaining will seem unmanly.

I feel that my only worth is in what I produce.

As in Phil's situation, a demon torturing supermen is the internalized belief that their self-worth is based on their ability to produce. This is often mirrored by some women in our society (e.g., the previously mentioned wife of the quarterback in the film *Any Given Sunday*). While many women are quick to say they see the worth of men for more than their economic abilities, many of those same women often cite the lack of eligible men as a problem of status and income. The term "good man" often has as much to do with a man's earning capacity as it does with his sensitivity, spiritual development, etc. So it is easy to see why so many men feel their worth is directly tied to their ability to produce. This can be a big hang-up issue in a relationship. If a man feels this way and he is unemployed or earns less than his mate, they can have problems. The key is for men to feel valued and important for more than their income, but that's easier said than done with all of the cues around us that imply the contrary.

I'm afraid that you love me for what I can do for you, not for who I am as a person.

Very closely related to the belief of self-worth being based on ability to produce is the fear that if he doesn't produce, he isn't worthy of the love of his woman. The hidden lover fears that his woman thinks of things that way too and he secretly fears that if he can't do anything for her, she'll view him as worthless and leave him for someone who can. For example, when a man is unemployed, underemployed, struggling financially, temporarily out of work due to illness, injury or long-term disability, he's in an extremely vulnerable place in his life because he feels inadequate. At such a time, reassurance from his woman that she loves him and believes in him can really bolster his confidence and will likely take his level of intimacy to a deeper place because he will realize that she in fact loves him for who he is as a person, not for what he does.

I'm exhausted from being the glue that holds everything together.

As stated earlier in the chapter, in the superman myth the man has to feel that he is the glue that holds everything together in his relationship. For example, he feels the sole responsibility to put food on the table and a roof overhead rests on his shoulders. If he has children, he feels it's his job to be the disciplinarian. With his wife (or girlfriend), he feels he has to be every possible thing she could want in a man. In essence, he's trying to be everything to everybody. What many men who feel they are the glue are afraid to say is that the role of trying to hold everything together is tearing them apart. On the outside, they may look like stalwart chisel-chin men of steel, but on the inside they're tired, frustrated and desperate for relief.

I want to break my normal routine and indulge in some rest and recreation.

Supermen, in their continuing quest to be everything to their wife, girlfriend or family, often wear themselves out physically, mentally and spiritually. I've known supermen who over the years have accumulated months of vacation time on jobs because they never go on vacations or even take time off. Some of them have had to be forced to go on vacation by their companies because they'd accumulated too much vacation time. Then there's the superman entrepreneur. These guys never take a break! Their work is their life. These guys always talk about how they're going to take a big vacation one day, a cruise or a long fishing trip. But that day never seems to come. For superman entrepreneurs, a break is simply doing less work, but working nonetheless.

What's interesting is that the supermen who won't take a break aren't always simply workaholics. They're under pressure, some of it self-imposed, but much of it real and imminent. But what I've learned in my own life is that you have to take a break or you'll come to a grinding halt and nothing will get accomplished. Things work in cycles and you can't function at your peak performance 100 percent of the time. For example, since I essentially give directly from my soul in my work, I find it easy to feel drained after a series of lectures or a book tour. Life has taught me the value of taking breaks and going on vacations. If I have to go fly a kite, go to the beach, work out or watch funny movies, I'll do it to shift my mind to a totally different gear. I have to do this or I am apt to slip into the role of the noble superman who tries to do everything for everybody, and I won't realize it until I've worn myself down.

THINGS TO THINK ABOUT

1. How much of a hidden lover's belief that he has to be superman is real and how much is self-imposed?
2. Do you think your man feels he has to be superman in order to meet your expectations?
3. Can you think of an example when your man tried to be a superman when he should've toned down, backed away or ignored something? What was the result?

JOURNAL ENTRY

At what times in your life have you played the role of super-woman? Reflect on this and delve into your reasons for doing this. You might consider writing about why you have been this way with specific individuals or in your approach to life as a whole. Consider these questions: What effect is being a superwoman having on your life, career and relationships? Can you continue to play this role? What will happen if you don't? How can you change this role and help those in your life adjust to a new you?

LETTER FROM A HIDDEN LOVER, PART 4

I'm always saying, "I'm not superman!" when I feel that I'm under too much pressure. But then even though I say that passionately, I turn right around and try to be superman because I feel that I have to.

A good example is when I really wanted to express to you how afraid I was when my company was going through those layoffs last year. My coworkers and I watched the ax fall on a different department every month. People we'd worked with for years were there, then suddenly they weren't. People with five, even ten years were being met at the door by security and escorted out with their possessions in a cardboard box. It was terrible. It was a time of high anxiety. I did tell you about it and we talked a lot about it. I mean it isn't as though I never brought it up. But I didn't ever tell you some of the more frightening information. And I never really let you know that I was on a list of people who were likely to be laid off or reclassified to lower-paying jobs in the company. Every day I prayed that I'd at least get to stay there until I could find another job. I read the classifieds at lunch every day, desperately searching for a new position.

I wanted to get some of the anxiety off my chest by talking to you but I felt that since I'm a man, I should handle my feelings better and not upset my woman. I didn't want to burden you with my fears so, instead of asking you for a listening and compassionate ear, I played superman.

I guess I was afraid you couldn't handle it, that you'd fall apart if you knew too much. And if you'd fallen apart on me at the time I would've lost my mind because I knew that if I lost my job we would've been in danger of losing the house and a whole lot more if I couldn't have found a new job in a couple of months. So I just didn't expose you to the daily drama of the rumor mill that was floating around the office. The pressure was killing me. I thought about going to the company's psychologist, but I was afraid that if somebody found out I was seeing a therapist at a time like that, I'd lose my job for sure.

I was also afraid that if I showed you how vulnerable I was feeling that you'd think less of me as a man. I was afraid you'd think that I wasn't handling things the way I should.

I can tell you now that those days were a time that almost broke me in half. I was having headaches and chest pains, and I even started thinking crazy stuff like that if I were laid off you'd start feeling that you'd be better off without me. Writing this part makes me want to cry. It was really tough for me through those days and I thank you for being there for me, even though I didn't let you be there for me as much as I wanted and needed you to. I did learn from that situation that I really don't want to play the role of superman anymore.

CHAPTER 5

THE HIDDEN LOVER NEEDS YOUR HELP BUT DOESN'T WANT TO ASK FOR IT

Since the hidden lover is often motivated by the belief that he has to play the role of superman, he rarely asks for help, even when he really needs it. A perfect illustration comes from an incident in my own life that happened last summer.

My wife and I enjoy entertaining and we often have friends and family over for backyard cookouts. We have three dogs and though we love them dearly, everyone who comes to our home isn't a dog lover. Therefore, we needed a place to put the dogs while entertaining; the solution was to build a fence across a section of the backyard behind the garage. After receiving outrageous quotes from fencing companies, I decided to do it myself. On a hot July afternoon, I began my hastily planned do-it-yourself project. After a quick trip to the hardware store, I was back home digging the post holes.

84

Within an hour my posts were set and I was starting the fence. I was hard at work when my wife came outside to see if I needed any help. I refused her help and brushed her away.

However she'd immediately noticed something that I'd missed. Since my project was planned and executed so quickly, I'd left the space for the gate too wide. She recommended that I take another look at it and consider putting the gateposts closer together. Being a hidden lover who didn't want to believe he needed any help, I summarily dismissed her opinion. But when the time came to install the gate, I realized she was right. Listening to her suggestion could've helped me avoid an error that involved another hour of digging and sawing. Afterward, I swallowed my pride and thanked her.

That's a comical example. Often things a man needs help on are far more serious, yet he still doesn't ask for help. Is a man any less of a man if he needs help solving problems, providing for his family or just asking for directions? The obvious answer is no. It's normal for a person to need help. But for hidden lovers, asking for help is a really big deal. Whether it's asking for directions on the interstate or asking his mate to give an opinion on a problem he's trying to solve, some men have a really hard time asking for help. Then there are those men who can ask for help on lots of things, except those that relate to health, financial challenges or relationship issues. Those are the men who will let everything go down the tubes before they will seek any help. But it's not because we're crazy. As I've emphatically stated before, the traditional role of men in this society has placed a demand on us to solve problems, give answers, and create solutions. Indeed, we treasure the ability to face a challenge and conquer it as a big part of being a man. And that's a good skill—until it goes overboard.

The truth is no man does anything alone. As the old adage says, "No man is an island." Nowhere is that more true than in our personal relationships. Relationships require emotional, financial, physical and spiritual sharing. They don't work well when one person feels more responsible for the preservation of the relationship than the other. Such a belief throws things out of balance. In relationships, the idea is not for one person to carry the load, but for two people to work together. A relationship is supposed to give us a healthy interdependence. Women seem to be more able to accept this. Why do men have so much trouble expressing their needs to their mate? Instead of saying they need help, men often act out their need for help in some of the following ways.

WAYS HIDDEN LOVERS ASK FOR HELP WITHOUT ACTUALLY ASKING: YOUR MAN MAY BE ASKING FOR HELP IF HE'S . . .

Continually mulling over a decision or idea in your presence

Rather than just coming out and asking for help, hidden lovers will use a technique known as "begging the question" to ask for help. In other words, they'll try to get you to offer to help them by making it clear they need help, without ever directly asking for help.

For example, if a hidden lover were contemplating applying for a new position, he might bring up the subject and then rattle off pros and cons. If he doesn't get any input the first time, he will try the technique over and over until he finally gets input. However, it usually doesn't take long for this technique to work successfully because most wives and girlfriends will offer their opinions readily upon hearing their man thinking aloud. The hidden lover realizes this and is often counting on it as a way of getting help without actually asking for it.

Remember, when a man is begging the question, he wants help. The basic idea is that if he didn't want your help, he wouldn't constantly mull over his ideas around you. He wouldn't even mention the ideas or thoughts he was contemplating if he didn't want input.

Disguising his true feelings as a joke

Another technique hidden lovers use to ask for help without dropping their masks of machismo is to mention an idea or feeling they have without owning up to it.

As an example, let's say a man and his family are going to the beach and the drive takes three hours. Let's say this man has worked harder than usual the past two weeks on a stressful project; he's been leaving before sunrise and getting home late in the evening. Yet he still feels compelled to drive the family to the beach. He'd like to ask his wife to drive there and back but he feels that it is his responsibility as the man to take the wheel. In his own way of asking for help, he might say, "Honey, I'm going to curl up in the back of the van and take a nap. Wake me when we get there." Immediately after saying that, he retracts his statement by saying, "I was just kidding."

Constantly complaining about the same issue

When a hidden lover is constantly complaining about the same thing, it's possible that somewhere in his complaint there's something he is trying to tell you about how you can help.

For example, suppose a hidden lover is constantly complaining that all the family needs is an additional thousand dollars a month of income in order to get out of debt. In doing this, he may be trying to bring up the delicate issue of income and expenses. Let's say, just for the sake of example, he's the primary income source in the home because his wife works part-time. His complaints may actually be his way of saying he wished she'd work full-time or more hours. Or he may be lodging a hidden complaint about her spending habits. He could also be grumbling because he feels overworked. Discerning if there's a hidden message in this situation takes highly attentive listening combined with not being overly sensitive.

Easily cranky / irritable

This call for help is probably obvious to many, but still needs to be mentioned. The word "help" isn't in the toolbox of many hidden lovers, but displaying displeasure with things through anger is a common tool of many men. Men often act out their hidden frustrations through anger that seems to come from nowhere. The hidden lover who is always grumbling and complaining is unhappy with something in his life and wants relief from it. The grumbling and complaining may be his way of asking for help, or at least expressing his pain. No doubt he wishes someone would pick up on the cue that he wants help.

TWO WAYS TO HELP A HIDDEN LOVER WHO WON'T ASK FOR HELP WHEN HE NEEDS IT

We have reviewed some of the ways hidden lovers ask for help without saying it. Now let's look at some ways to help a hidden lover, even when he may not ask. As you read these suggestions it is useful to remember a basic strategy. Try to understand that a man wants to feel he is solving his own problems. Even if a man receives help, he wants to feel that he is ultimately in charge of solving his own problems. This goes back to the feeling males have that being a man means being able to handle any and every thing from fighting off Goliath to a balancing a checkbook.

Here are two ways to help a man who needs help but won't ask for it:

Let him know you are willing to help.

There's nothing harder than watching a person struggle with a task that you could easily help them with, if he would allow it. Many women find themselves in this position when trying to help their hidden lovers. Unfortunately, the only thing to do is to offer help and then back off. This is important because he will not take persistent offers to help him as sympathy, but rather as nagging. With the hidden lover it is necessary to give him the space to see that he needs help. Ironically, you've already helped simply by offering your help. Having done that, you've helped him by allowing him to know help is there when and if he needs it. At some point, he'll ask for it, directly or indirectly.

Let him find out he needs help.

Men often have to try it their way before asking for any help. Some men feel it's necessary to exhaust all options before asking for help. As long as they aren't causing danger or extreme inconvenience to anyone else, this can be a chance for them to learn the value of asking for the help and assistance of others.

A good opportunity for this happens every day in cars all

across America. A man thinks he knows where he's going, won't ask for directions and gets lost. If your man insists on doing this over and over, be sure to get yourself a good reliable cell phone! Then when he gets lost for lack of asking for directions, let him make the call to find out how to correct his mistake; or let him be the one asking someone for directions. Then when you get where you're going, give him a look that says, "Don't ever do that again." He'll get the point.

Considering the aforementioned, here's an important footnote.

You don't have to play dumb!

Please understand, I'm explaining the way many men think. I'm in no way suggesting that women simply bat their eyes, smile and play dumb while a man makes an obvious error in judgment. My intention here is for women to get an understanding of what so many guys are thinking but aren't saying when it comes to asking for help. Then for the sake of peace and progress, they can help these men see that it is okay to be helped. Suggestions to men are definitely one of those things better offered with sugar than salt. But never play dumb in order to stroke his ego. Playing dumb doesn't help any. It just lets him continue to think he knows everything when he doesn't, which is something he needs to unlearn for his own sake as well as that of your relationship.

TYPES OF WOMEN WHO MAKE HIDDEN LOVERS AVOID ASKING FOR HELP

As a final note, it's important to mention that it's not just male ego that prevents some hidden lovers from asking for help. When it comes to asking, one important thing to know is that some men don't feel they can open up to their mates because they don't feel it is safe to do so. Consider the following women and why hidden lovers wouldn't feel safe asking them for any kind of help.

Helpless Helena

Helpless Helena is depending on her man to save the day. She says she's just an old-fashioned girl, but that's really a cover for the fact that she has no emotional strength. Her man can't ask her for any help because she'll crumble at the very idea that he isn't strong enough to handle any and every thing.

Bossy Belinda

Men who are involved with Bossy Belinda can't ask her for help because she'll pounce on them like a bird on a bug. Instead of being a comforter, she'll find fault in what he says or thinks. He'll wish he never brought it up in the first place.

Selfish Stacy

This woman will listen to a man who says he needs help, but she doesn't care. For Selfish Stacy the relationship is all about how she feels and what she wants. The man who tries to confide in her will only be hurt when he realizes she really doesn't care.

Emotional Edna

There's one good thing to say about Emotional Edna—she cares; and she doesn't mind letting a man know that she cares. The problem with her is that she's like Helpless Helena, only worse. She flies into histrionics when she's confronted with a problem. She falls apart if a man tells her anything because she can't handle it.

Vicious Vivian

Vicious Vivian is the woman who is looking for a way to trump her man, always trying to get one up on him. Like her Bossy cousin, Belinda, Vicious Vivian will use a man's need for help as a way to slam him. For her, the relationship is a competition. Finding out that he needs help is seen as a way for her to get one up on him. She may help him, but only with a dubious motive.

Mean Melissa

Mean Melissa doesn't have any compassion. If the man in her life turns to her for help, instead of being a shoulder to lean on, she'll deeply insult him. She'll say something such as "Why don't you stop whining?" Or "Shut up. Be a man!"

THINGS TO THINK ABOUT

1. Does your man have difficulty asking for help?
2. Are there some things that are asking too much when it comes to a man asking his woman for help? If yes, what are they and why are those things asking for too much?
3. What is a healthy level of sharing and helping in a relationship?

JOURNAL ENTRY

Jot down a few thoughts about a time in a relationship when you know your man needed your help but he wouldn't ask for it. How did that make you feel? What is his response when you try to help him? Does he accept help for some things, but not others? What do you think motivates this behavior?

A LETTER FROM THE HIDDEN LOVER, PART 5

Me, ask for help? Sure, I know I need help sometimes, and certainly there are times I know I should ask for your help. So why don't I just ask you to help me when I feel I need your help?

Actually I do ask for your help. I ask for your help on a lot of things, but I just don't ask using words. I guess sometimes I just try to get you to see that I need help without saying it. I try to act a certain way or leave you clues. One way I ask for help is that I'll be unusually silent and wait for you to ask if something's wrong. That's one way you can tell. But the best way you can tell that I'm in a situation in which I need help is those times when I'm really prickly to be around and I seem to get easily upset or disturbed about the smallest little things you do. When I'm acting that way, I feel you'll know there's something wrong. The only problem is that doing this usually makes it seem that I'm angry at you when that isn't always the case.

Usually if I'm really angry at you then I just clam up and get away from you. So if I'm around you acting funny, I probably actually want you to notice my behavior so you'll ask me what's wrong because it's not something that has to do with our relationship.

You could chalk it up to pride or you could say I'm being

silly. But the fact of the matter is that I'm not comfortable asking you for help—at least not on things I feel I should deal with in a manly way. You see, part of me is stuck in the belief that I, as the man, shouldn't be asking for help. I believe I should be a strong provider and protector and that you should be able to come to me for help. But then another part of me says that even a man who is a strong provider and protector sometimes needs help.

But I do need help and I'm glad that I get it from you. Secretly, I'm glad that we share the expenses. I'm glad you have a good job and you're able to help take care of us. That takes a great burden off my mind. Since you have a career too, I don't have to worry about what we'd do if I were ill, or laid off. I know that I often discourage you from working overtime, but when you pick up those extra hours, it sure helps. I guess the man in me is split: part of me wants you to be able to stay home and be queen of the castle, but the more practical side of me wants to have a mate who is working and helping us achieve our goals.

Money isn't the only issue. I often want help with emotional issues, but don't ask for it. One such time was when I had that big fall-out with my best friend, Barry, over which one of us made our team lose the game. You didn't know we practically came to blows that night at the basketball court. That whole day was a bad day. I had a bad day at work. Then I went to play basketball to let off some steam. Both Barry and I were playing lousy for some reason. Maybe he was having a bad day too. Then he missed the winning shot and we lost. He says it was because I gave him a bad pass. I unloaded on him. We locked horns and got in each other's faces. Then I came home angry but didn't say anything to you about it. When I saw you in the bedroom reading, I almost told you what happened but I didn't want to seem like a big crybaby so I made a sandwich and plopped down on the couch to watch television. That's why when you said something to me about not wiping my feet when I came through the living room, I went off on you. Then we were angry at each other all night.

Looking back on it, that was a time I wanted and needed help and should've asked for it. The help I wanted was just a compassionate heart to hear me. But instead of asking for help, in the form of your listening to me, I shut you out as though you were a part of the problem. I didn't mean it to come off that way. But that's the way it happened.

So that's something else I wanted to tell you. I do need your help a lot more than I may say.

CHAPTER 6

HOW FEAR OF LOSING FREEDOM AFFECTS THE HIDDEN LOVER

Recently, when I was taking a seminar, during a break I overheard two of the men in the group talking. Before I heard exactly what these guys were discussing, I knew the subject. See if you can guess what they were talking about.

The first man said, "Man, I just can't see myself doing it. I mean . . . I just don't know if I could deal with it."

The other guy said, "Yeah. I don't understand how some guys can do it. It's too hard to juggle that with your career and having your own life too."

"It seems like a prison sentence."

Have you guessed the subject of this conversation yet? After the last comment, I walked over and said, "You two guys must be talking about marriage." They both broke into laughter.

But is it really funny? Or should it be a cause of concern that some men have hidden feelings of marriage and commitment being like a prison sentence? It's interesting to note that these were successful, thirty-something, professional men, so-called good catches. Yet they were cynical about marriage. Listening to their words closely, it didn't seem as though they were particularly cynical about relationships or marriage; but more so about an idea of certain things that would come along with it. This isn't an isolated situation; many hidden lovers I've interviewed, both single (in relationships) and married, describe relationships in such a way that it sounds as though they feel they are prisoners—a man's worst nightmare. The fear of losing his freedom is a major source of problems for the hidden lover because *men value having a feeling of freedom, even in a relationship.*

I'm sure in reality, if you could be a fly on the wall, you'd find that some of the guys are bellyaching about nothing but imagined problems. You'd find that others are just too lazy (emotionally or otherwise) to give of themselves at the level required in a relationship. But you'd also find some guys who are genuinely serving out a term in a relationship that is in fact like a prison sentence.

Now ladies, please don't get sensitive. In this book I promised to deliver the thoughts and fears of hidden lovers in an effort to improve relationships even when the information isn't very palatable. Any discussion of the hidden feelings of men would be incomplete without the issue of the fear men have about losing their freedom to a relationship. In fact, a Virginia Slims Opinion Poll reported that 61 percent of men surveyed rated "being independent" as the number-one "very important" thing in defining who they are.

Therefore, let's look at the concerns of hidden lovers that if left unchecked can make a relationship start to feel like a ball and chain. I interviewed men to find out what those issues and concerns were and have reported them here. The following comments in quotes are actually composites gathered from interviews with a diverse group of men. The composites represent the general tone of what they said.

I FEEL I'M LOSING MY FREEDOM WHEN . . .

My wife/girlfriend asks me to pick up something for her every time I go somewhere.

"Sometimes I just want to go out somewhere and do something for myself without having to stop at the store to pick up milk or something."

This was a common response from hidden lovers. They felt that their significant other was always asking them to stop and get something from the store or run an errand while they were out. Of course there's nothing inherently wrong with that. But if it happens all the time, it can be irritating at the

least, and at worst make a man feel he doesn't have freedom
to leave the house without paying the toll of having to perform
a "honey-do" task. Perhaps an example would bring this out
better.

Josh is sitting at home and he decides he wants a Sunday
paper. He's in a leisurely mood and feels carefree and
relaxed. All he wants to do is read the paper for an hour. He
gets up and calls across the room to his wife, "Honey, I'm
going to get a paper."

"Oh good, you're going to the store. Will you pick up a few
things?"

In her mind, there's absolutely nothing wrong with this
statement. She figures: he's going to the store; surely he won't
mind picking up a few things. On the other hand, he's thinking: all I wanted to do was just get a paper, come home and
read. Now I've got to start shopping. For him, this is an intru-
sion into his leisure. He may very well be the kind of man
who will do any and everything for his wife; but at the
moment he just wants to go get a paper and read. Anything
beyond that is seen as a nuisance.

Should a woman be able to ask her man to pick up things
from the store? Of course! The complaint wasn't that men were
asked to do something, it was that some of them felt it happened too much. As I stated earlier, it really isn't as much
about the errand as it is about the mode of thinking the man
was in at the moment. He wanted to do one thing and then
come home. It's not unusual for men to be single-minded

about tasks. On the other hand, women seem to like to do several things at once, or at least are better at it. For example, if my wife is out grocery shopping and running two or three errands, I can ask her to pick up something for me and it's usually no big deal to her. While for me, such a request would feel like too much to add to what I already had focused in my mind to do.

She tries to plan what I'm going to do on my off days.

"The night before my off day, my wife starts giving me lists of things to do and it drives me up the wall."

This is a big one. It feels like a direct denial of a man's freedom. A responsible man doesn't mind running errands or doing odd jobs around the house because he knows they need to be done. But he resents his wife or girlfriend taking charge of his off days with an agenda she's put together for him. Here's an example:

FRED: Guess what, Doris?

DORIS: What, honey?

FRED: The boss gave everybody tomorrow off.

DORIS: Wonderful, I didn't know you had tomorrow off. [She starts to ponder.]

FRED (turning on the television): I guess I'll put in a movie. Since I'm off tomorrow I can sleep in.

DORIS: Sweetie, while you're off tomorrow can you
  look at the washer? It's making that whirring sound
  again. Also, I'd really appreciate it if you would
  drop me off at work in the morning and take my
  car to get a tune-up. You might as well wash and
  vacuum it while you have it. Then around three
  can you go by my sister's house and pick up the
  casserole dish I left over there last week?

FRED (looking disgusted): Maybe I should call my
  boss and see if I can go to work tomorrow so I can
  have a day off from home!

Is Fred partly responsible for those chores as a member
of the relationship? Definitely! But do they all have to be
done on his off day? What things were major and needed to
be done and which could wait so he could enjoy his bonus
day off? What Doris doesn't realize is that Fred feels she's
invading his space.

She thinks something's wrong if I want to go out with my friends.

"My girlfriend thinks we're supposed to spend all of our spare
time together. It's a real drain on me."

Relationships require a sharing of time. Moreover, people
in relationships should naturally want to spend time together.
However, they should have their own friends and activities

outside of each other. Relationships gain when both individuals have a healthy and rounded life outside the relationship. Resentment builds quickly in men who feel their relationship requires them to be cut off from the outside world. This is one of the most feared ball-and-chain scenarios for the hidden lover.

She constantly calls and pages me.

"My girlfriend makes me feel like I don't have a life of my own. She calls me all the time at work, in the car and at home. It seems she calls me every five!"

There's no better way to make a man feel as though he's lost his freedom to a relationship than to call him and page him all the time. Some men feel as though this is a way women attempt to keep tabs on them. In some cases that's true. But I don't think it's always that sinister. Women like to have connection. They may just want to see if their man is all right or check what kind of day he's having. But men, desiring autonomy, sometimes interpret such calls as a woman trying to keep tabs on them or resent her being too dependent.

In this case what couples need is a way to deal with this issue that satisfies a man's need for autonomy and a woman's need for connection. Sounds complicated, but it's not impossible.

For example, when I arrived at school one day to teach classes, I didn't realize the schedule had been changed and my classes weren't meeting that morning. With my free time, I decided to run some errands. I went to get a haircut. Then I picked up a new suit from a tailor who was doing alterations on it. I stopped at a bookstore to see the new releases and sign some of my books that were in stock. I grabbed a sandwich at a deli. Then I stopped at the gym for a quick workout. When I'd finished all of those things, it was two hours later than I normally returned home. No sooner had I thought about that than my wife called on the cell phone.

She was calling to see if everything was all right since I hadn't come home at my normal time. She also asked me why I hadn't called so she wouldn't be worried. That was a good question. I suppose the answer was that being a man, I don't like to feel as though I'm giving reports on all of my where-abouts. It makes me feel as though I've lost my independence.

But I should've called. If I think about it from her point of view, it makes sense. If my wife were out two hours later than her regular time coming home I'd want her to call so I'd know everything was all right.

Tact in such situations is the key. As a woman, she wants to connect. As a man, I want to feel independent. The best thing to do is just casually discuss the events of the day. That way she doesn't have to ask an awkward question such as "Where have you been?" and I don't have to feel as though I'm being questioned. It's all about respecting the other person's needs and feelings. Here are some things to keep in mind next time you face this situation:

What Not to Say or Do (Men)

1. Never make your absence a mystery by offering no details.
2. Never say things such as, "Don't ask me where I've been."

What Not to Say or Do (Women)

1. Don't ask for minute-by-minute details of everything your husband/boyfriend did that day.
2. Don't crossexamine him.
3. Never say threatening things such as, "You'd better have a good excuse."

She scolds me for the clothes I want to wear.

"Sometimes I feel like I'm in grade school. Some mornings my wife actually lays my clothes out for me."

Sinbad, one of my favorite comedians, has a hilarious skit he does about a man and his children who are waiting for his wife to lay their clothes out on the bed. Part of the act is to pick men out of the audience who he says have obviously been dressed by their wives. We often laugh at comedians because their humor is such a mirror of real life. Apparently this situation is true of enough men to make an audience burst into laughter.

On one hand, this isn't a bad idea. My wife has excellent taste in clothing; I have none. My wife has saved me on many occasions from getting a citation from the fashion police. Before that, I guess people were just whispering about me or saying, Poor man, he obviously doesn't have help getting dressed.

But when taken to an extreme, a woman's fashion directions for a man can feel like a loss of freedom. It's one thing for a woman to suggest clothing to her mate. But to be insulting, insistent or pestering about it can lead to the feeling of being tied to a ball and chain. Sure, you should try to persuade him not to wear his favorite five-year-old faded green Polo shirt to the company picnic. But don't micromanage every phase of his wardrobe.

She asks me whom I was talking to when I get off the phone.

"I don't feel like I have any privacy to make phone calls."

There are two ways people ask their significant other whom they are talking to on the phone: inquisitively—simply curious and done with respect; and suspiciously—implying that there's something secretive going on. There's nothing wrong with sincere inquiries about whom your man is talking to on the phone. The problem is with suspicious inquiries such as the following.

One man confided that his wife goes so far as to monitor his calls. When he and his wife both answer the phone at the same time, she fakes a hang-up and stays on the phone to find out who's on the other end of the line. When confronted with this, she denies it or says the phone must have been off the hook without her knowledge.

She tries to poke into my business affairs.

"She overheard me talking to an associate on the phone about some plans we were making for a deal. When I hung up she started telling me how I should run my own business."

A man's work is critical to his self-esteem. This is an area in which many men derive much of their self-worth. Therefore, if his significant other is constantly second-guessing his business decisions, he will probably take it personally. He may take it to mean that she is saying he is not capable of doing his job as a man because he can't take care of business. In fact, that's why men are sensitive about this area. But this doesn't mean that a woman shouldn't point out a good idea when she has one. And it doesn't mean that men don't consult their wives and girlfriends about business—because they do all the time. But if she's always looking over his shoulder and second-guessing him, it's going to have a negative effect on how he feels about the relationship.

In conclusion, I can't emphasize enough how important it is for a man to have a feeling of autonomy and freedom, even within a relationship. Losing the feeling of freedom makes even the best husbands and boyfriends start to feel boxed in, and that feeling becomes a source of significant problems for him. Without a feeling of freedom and autonomy a man will retreat within himself and become a hidden lover.

THINGS TO THINK ABOUT

1. What makes you feel that you've lost the freedom to have your own life or be yourself in a relationship?
2. How can a couple mutually assure that they respect each other's freedom and autonomy while still having a close relationship?
3. What are healthy boundaries for people in a relationship?

JOURNAL ENTRY

Have you ever been in a relationship in which you feel someone is limiting your freedom or draining your energy by placing too many demands on you? If so, how? What did you do that allowed the problem to continue? How would you avoid being in that situation again? If you're in such a situation, what are the issues you'd like to bring up to your mate to change the situation?

LETTER FROM THE HIDDEN LOVER, PART 6

This may sound crazy to you. But although I love being married and having a family, I also love being alone or getting away from my family. I suppose it's a guy thing, but I have to have my freedom.

The other night when I was over at Barry's house watching a football game, you called. Before I could get to the phone all the guys were making jokes and laughing. They were cracking all these "honey-do" jokes. That's okay because I can handle them. But the worst part of it was that it was true. You wanted me to stop at the store to get some bread and apples. Now don't get me wrong, I don't mind doing that most of the time. But what you didn't understand was that I was on my "man time," that precious time when I want to feel as though I'm wild and free, even if it is just for a few hours a week. So though picking up a loaf of bread and some apples isn't a tall order, it's enough to destroy the vibe of what "man time" is all about because it immediately makes me feel like I'm domesticated when I'm trying to be wild. It's just a guy thing.

When I seemed a little curt with you I could tell you were offended. You said, "Well excuse me! Just forget it, I'll never ask you to pick up anything again!" Then you hung up in my face.

I said "Bye" so it wouldn't be obvious that you'd just hung up on me because I would've never lived that down. I walked back through the room of guys, who made all of their jokes again. Especially Ray and Vic. Ray would say, "Honey, can you do this?" Then Vic would say, "Honey, can you do that?" They did it through a commercial break. Then as fate would have it, Vic's wife called on his cell phone and I got my revenge.

I guess the bottom line is that I want to feel that I have freedom. I'm not saying I want to go out and screw around with other women. I'm not talking about walking in the house at any hour of the night and your not even being allowed to ask where I've been. I'm not even talking about how you often call me a couple of times during the day just to touch base. It's more about the spirit of freedom. Because if a guy feels he's on a ball and chain, he's going to freak out in some way. That's one of the big fears men have about getting married in the first place; the fear that they'll lose themselves to matrimony. Below I've listed a few things I'd like to do, with your blessing. These things will keep me from feeling like I'm on a ball and chain in our marriage.

1. Don't sweat me about going places alone, like fishing or hanging out with the guys.
2. When I'm out with the guys, or on my "man time," don't call unless it's an emergency. Just let me be alone for a while.

3. Leave one place in the house where I don't have the usual rules. I need a space to call my own that I can set up to my liking and retreat to as my cave.

4. Leave the toilet seats up. (Just kidding, I know that's asking too much!)

CHAPTER 7

THE HIDDEN LOVER'S NEED
FOR APPRECIATION
AND RESPECT

Everyone likes to be appreciated and treated with respect. But for the hidden lover, being appreciated and respected equates to how loved he feels. However, this can be a touchy issue today. We live in a time of extreme political correctness; therefore, men asking to be "appreciated and respected" may feel they run the risk of appearing to be chauvinistic or patriarchal. Therefore, they're often hesitant to express to their wives and girlfriends exactly how important it is to them that they are appreciated and respected.

Please note that in referring to appreciation and respect, I'm not referring to women bowing down and kissing our feet. That's not where I'm going. This chapter was written to help women identify some of the things that women can inadvertently do to make a man feel unappreciated and disrespected, and thus cause him to be a hidden lover.

ACTIONS THAT MAKE HIDDEN LOVERS FEEL UNAPPRECIATED

There are some things a woman can do that are guaranteed to make a man feel unappreciated and marginalized. The following are things that can really dampen a man's self-esteem in a relationship; and it's important to reiterate here that when a man doesn't feel appreciated, he feels unloved. Where this is particularly important in relating to the hidden lover is that he is already tucked away in his shell like a turtle. If he feels he's being unappreciated and marginalized, he will never feel it's safe to be the man he really desires to be in the relationship.

Not recognizing his work achievements

I can't overemphasize how important a man's work is to his feeling of worth. I'm not saying it's the optimal way of self-definition, but it's nonetheless true. Even as I write these words, I realize I'm no different. Men largely define their self-worth through their work.

Therefore, if you don't recognize or acknowledge your man's work achievements, he feels you don't appreciate him or respect who he is. Women who really want to get a good inside track on intimacy with a man make an effort to notice and acknowledge his work achievements. This could be something simple, such as telling him you appreciate how hard he works. Or it could be asking him about his work and showing a sincere interest in what he does. Another idea is to ask him if you can visit his job so he can show you what he does.

Comparing him unfavorably to other men

Men are competitive, maybe even too much so in some situations. Unfortunately, we see almost everything in life as a game of King of the Hill in which there is no second place—it's winner take all.

Therefore, when a woman compares a man unfavorably to other men, he feels threatened. His first response may be to trivialize the other man. Or he may start pointing out faults in the other man while stressing areas of his superiority. It's important to understand that the comparison doesn't have to be about muscles or income; it can be about almost anything. The key is that he's being sized up against another man and therefore feels the necessity to feel superior to him or to at least measure up to him.

NOTE: I want to stress that such thinking isn't necessarily the best way for a man to live his life. Seeing everything in life as a constant winner-take-all competition is a sure route to stress and possibly self-destruction.

Favoring the advice of others over his advice

Just as being compared unfavorably to other men makes a man feel bad, men also feel bad when their advice is routinely ignored by their significant other. At issue isn't so much whether a man's significant other follows his advice, but whether she makes him feel that his advice is important. If she listens to his advice, he feels that he has been appreciated and valued. But if she summarily dismisses him as not knowing what he is talking about, he feels unappreciated and devalued. An example of this was mentioned in the last chapter. Here's another example to elaborate on the issue further.

Fred's girlfriend Gina was having car problems. Fred had diagnosed the problem to be something related to the fuel system. His hunch was that it was probably the carburetor. The next day, Gina called her uncle and asked him to look at the car. He told Gina the car needed a new fuel filter. Gina believed him and had total confidence in his opinion. When Gina brought this up to Fred he got angry. He was angry because she so quickly believed what someone else, particularly another man, had to say, over his opinion. Regardless of whether he was wrong or right, Fred felt unappreciated and disrespected.

Not believing in him

One of the strongest affirmations a man can receive from his woman is for her to simply say, "I believe in you." Those words fill a man with strength and power. When she says those words he knows she trusts him and she feels that he is capable of protecting and providing for her (in whatever form or capacity relevant to their relationship). Saying those words is the verbal equivalent to a woman laying her head on a man's chest. When a man feels his woman doesn't "believe in her man" he feels inadequate to the degree that it will threaten the foundation of the relationship.

TRIGGER WORDS AND PHRASES

It's also important to look at the role of words said by a woman to a man. A wife or girlfriend can say something that can derail her man for the rest of the day. Some things she says can penetrate so deeply that a man will never really forget the words and always be hurt by them. It seems as though women have an intuitive sense of just what to say to press a man's buttons. Such trigger words and phrases are painful because they strike deep inside at a man's sense of self-esteem.

Telling him he acts like a little boy

Calling a man a "little boy" with intent to chastise him presses a man's buttons. A man doesn't want to be called a boy because that implies that he is immature and incapable of handling things. This is taken as a direct assault on his manhood.

Telling him he's whining

Accusing a man of whining is taken by the man to mean that he's not man enough to rise to the occasion. When told he's whining, what a man hears is that he's being told he's not acting like a "real" man—the underlying point being that a "real" man will take action when facing a challenge, while wimps tuck tail and whine.

Telling him to "be a man"

Ouch! This one really stings. When a woman fires these words at a man she can be sure that he has been wounded. It hurts so much because his *woman* is telling her man that he isn't being a man. He feels she's telling him he's inadequate in the role of man. Few things can hurt like those words.

Calling him a "punk" or a "sissy"

This is one degree more severe than telling him to be a man. No heterosexual man wants to be called a "punk" or a "sissy" by a woman. Such words from a woman make a heterosexual man feel emasculated because he is somewhat dependent upon his woman's affirmation of his very manhood. This may sound homophobic or like insecurity to some people, but it's not. Even the most liberal-thinking heterosexual man wants to be identified as heterosexual because it's a large part of who he is.

Telling him he's "lazy and no good for anything"

This is an old one but no less effective today. Telling a man he's worthless cuts him down to nothing because he bases so much of his worth on being an asset to his significant other and his family. Telling him he's worthless is tantamount to letting the air out a balloon. It is a terrible assault on his self-esteem.

I hope after reading this list women understand the severity of these verbal body blows and refrain from using them. Even in a heated argument, they aren't going to help. They'll only throw gasoline on the fire. Moreover, these words can only cause rifts in a relationship. Most, if not all of them, will leave lasting emotional wounds and resentment.

HENPECKING

Verbal chides are another area of sensitivity for hidden lovers. Painful words and verbal attacks of various forms fall into the realm of henpecking. I define henpecking as an attempt to gain influence over a man by whining, complaining or nagging with the intent of wearing a man down until he is in agreement with a woman's wishes. Henpeckers have various motives. But their intentions, whether good or dubious, are driving their men crazy. Henpecking makes a man want to be anywhere but with a henpecker. He'll work longer hours, find afterwork activities or do anything to avoid her grinding away at his soul with constant whining, complaining, bickering and nagging.

Henpecking comes in five degrees, the lowest degree being whining.

Whining is saying things in a tone that grates directly on a man's nerves. It often goes hand in hand with begging. Whining is the most passive level of henpecking because it can be most easily ignored.

Complaining is more aggressive than whining but is still a passive form of henpecking because it stops short of personal insults. A skilled complainer doesn't have to use insults because her complaining is often enough motivation to spur even the most stubborn man into action.

Bickering is similar to complaining, except it's more

aggressive. A bickering type knows she's getting on a man's nerves but doesn't care. Bickering is her weapon and she knows how to use it. Bickering types even seem to enjoy being annoying.

Nagging is intentionally aggressive. The nagger is abrasive and callous and doesn't mind being that way to get what she wants. There's no doubt that she enjoys making personal insults, put-downs and taunts.

In the following examples, the difference between whining, complaining, bickering and nagging are illustrated. In each of the dialogues between Alan and Nikki, the subject is the same, but the approaches are different. Which one would irk you the most? How would you approach the situation differently?

Whining

NIKKI: Alan, you've been sitting out for an hour just staring at the stars. Is there something wrong?

ALAN: No, I'm just thinking.

NIKKI: What are you thinking about?

ALAN: Just thinking. . . . Lots of things.

NIKKI: Share your thoughts with me.

ALAN: I don't really feel like talking.

NIKKI (her voice droning): You said that last time you were doing this. Why won't you share your thoughts with me?

ALAN (becoming irritated): There's nothing to share at
the moment. I'm just thinking in general.

NIKKI (in a droning singsong voice): How can we be
a couple if you won't share your thoughts with me?

ALAN (getting up and marching into the house): I
can't stand it when you start that whining!

NIKKI (angry): I'm not whining!

Complaining

NIKKI: Alan, you've been sitting out here staring at
the sky long enough. It's been almost an hour.
What are you thinking about?

ALAN: Lots of things.

NIKKI: Like what?

ALAN: Just things . . . Sweetheart, can we talk later? I
just want to think right now.

NIKKI: I don't see why whatever you're thinking
about is so important that you can't share it with
me.

ALAN: That's not the point.

NIKKI (angry): I guess I'm just not that important to
you anymore.

ALAN: I didn't say that.

NIKKI: You don't have to. If you cared about me
you'd invite me to sit down with you. I don't see
why you do this anyway. It's a waste of time.

ALAN: I just want some time alone to think and let my mind relax. Is that a problem?

NIKKI: If you want to sit and think, why don't you go fishing? Then at least you'd have something to show for all this time.

ALAN (walking toward the house): Forget it.

NIKKI: Where are you going?

ALAN (spinning around to face Nikki): If you're going to complain about me sitting outside on the deck, I'll just go in and watch television with you.

NIKKI: Don't get angry. I just asked you what you were thinking.

Bickering

NIKKI: Why are you sitting out here staring up at the sky?

ALAN: Just thinking.

NIKKI: About what?

ALAN: Lots of things.

NIKKI (with an edge in her voice): Like what?

ALAN: Just lots of things. Nothing in particular.

NIKKI: Oh, I see. You just don't want to talk to me about what's on your mind. I'm good enough to share your bed, but I'm not good enough to share your thoughts.

ALAN: What did you say?

NIKKI: You heard me. You think you can have it all your way. I ask you a simple question and then you act like you can't answer it. All I wanted to know was what you were thinking about and you started becoming secretive.

ALAN (sarcastically): Okay, sit down and lets talk about any and everything that's on my mind. Every time a thought pops into my head, I'll tell you. I hope you have all evening!

NIKKI: Very funny. If you're going to have an attitude about it, forget it!

Nagging

NIKKI: Have you lost your mind? You've been staring up at the sky for an hour. What are you thinking about?

ALAN: Lots of things.

NIKKI: What in the world could be so important that you have to sit out there looking at the moon? Are you going to start howling like a wolf in a minute? Maybe I'd better call the Animal Control Department.

ALAN: Like I said, I'm not thinking about anything important, I'm just thinking, letting my mind wander.

NIKKI: Well, you could let your mind wander toward

getting a head start on writing out next month's bills if you want something to think about. Or you could let your mind wander toward how we're going to get that old car of yours fixed. Or what you're going to do about our son's grades in math. I've got plenty you can think about instead of just staring into the sky and thinking about nothing.

ALAN (throwing up his hands and walking into the house): I'm going to bed. Hopefully I won't have nightmares about my nagging wife.

NIKKI: Nagging you? I'm not nagging you. I just gave you some things that needed to be thought about around here since you seemed to be thinking about nothing.

ALAN: You can be impossible to deal with.

THINGS TO THINK ABOUT

1. When was the last time you told your man something you appreciate about him. For example, "I appreciate how hard you work."
2. Why do you think people forget to show appreciation for their mate?

JOURNAL ENTRY

List the things you would like your man to appreciate about you. Do you think he is aware of these things and how you feel about them? What things do you think he wants to be appreciated for? Why? Based on the writings in your journal, discuss these things with him to increase your mutual appreciation of each other.

A LETTER FROM THE HIDDEN LOVER, PART 7

It's really important to me that I feel appreciated and valued in your life. I do feel that you appreciate me. But I want you to understand just how important that is to me. This example will show you what I mean. Since last Christmas, I've been walking around with some hidden resentment about a time I didn't feel you appreciated me. Not only did it hurt my feelings, this particular incident felt publicly humiliating to me.

Last Christmas we were at the Hendersons' party and we were talking with two other couples about how to download a certain type of computer file from the Internet. It was one of those little funny animations that we all wanted because we'd heard so much about it. One of the couples was listening because they said they didn't know how to do it. But the guy from the other couple, Jerry, Mr. Loudmouth, was talking as though he knew how to do it. I knew what Jerry was saying was wrong because we'd already downloaded the file at work and Jerry was missing a couple of steps in his directions, so I disagreed with him and told him the proper way to download the file.

Meanwhile, Mr. Loudmouth's wife was agreeing with her husband. But instead of agreeing with me, you thought Jerry was right. You just flew into agreement with them as though I didn't have a clue. I felt you had no appreciation for my opinion. I felt that you didn't value anything I said and that made me feel pretty worthless. Then, to make matters worse, you started reinterpreting everything I was saying so it didn't sound as though I was in contention with Jerry. It still makes me angry a year later.

What I wished you would've done in that situation was listen to me and take my opinion as seriously as you did Jerry's. I felt at the moment that you had fallen victim to the habit some wives have of taking their husband's opinion for granted and instead always seeking someone else's opinion. That's a place I never want to be. I've seen couples like that and they're really sad to me. They always doubt each other's ideas and opinions. We're not like that and I don't want to get that way because it is a breeding ground for problems when a couple doesn't have the utmost appreciation and respect for one another.

That's why that night bothered me so much. I remember drifting off into the crowd shortly after that. I mingled with people and drank my punch while inside I continued to simmer. You seemed to sense something was wrong and asked me. I said, "I don't know, why don't you ask, Jerry?" That's when you kind of rolled your eyes playfully and gave me a hug. To you the issue was resolved. But for me, it had cut more deeply than I think you realized.

Finally I let it go. But I didn't erase it altogether. I just moved it to a back burner. And that's what I'm trying to get over. I'm trying to stop hiding these sorts of things because they just become sources of arguments and blowups later. That's why I'm telling you about it in this letter. The big point isn't even the party. The main issue is that as a man I really need to feel appreciated and supported by my woman. It means a lot to me.

CHAPTER 8

THE HIDDEN LOVER'S VIEWS ON SEX

He's Not Like All the Other Guys

The hidden lover wants you to know that when it comes to sex, he isn't like all of the other guys. He isn't obsessed with sex the way the stereotype of the typical man in the beer commercials suggests. Hidden lovers have moved beyond sex being their primary motivation for everything they do with women. This isn't to say that they don't immensely enjoy sex. Nor is this to suggest that they don't have the spontaneous random thoughts that other men have about sex, because they do. But they've come to a point in their lives at which they aren't slaves to their sex drive. It's important to the hidden lover to make this known to his partner. He wants her to realize that he's different from the stereotypical man. This chapter will express some of the hidden lover's feelings and views on sex.

THE BASICS ON MEN AND SEX

Fact: It's not accurate to lump us all into the "men" category when it comes to sex. When it comes to viewpoints on sex, all men are not the same. Sometimes we see things differently because of our relationship status. For example, single guys generally tend to have sex on the brain more than men in long-term relationships or marriage. Why? Mainly because a single guy in the dating world may go in and out of sexual relationships (no pun intended) without actually having the responsibilities that come with a relationship. In other words, married men or men in committed relationships have a broader relationship with a woman that encompasses much more than sex. They're also concerned with the economics of a relationship, the feelings involved and numerous other day-to-day realities. They have deep emotional ties and real responsibilities to each other that come with co-existing with another person as an intimate part of their lives; it's a totally different reality. Therefore, sex isn't the only thing they share and it isn't their primary way of relating to each other.

Another big factor affecting the way individual men view sex is the man's age and maturity level. Young guys have turbo-charged hormones and can't seem to think about relationships except in terms of sex. But when a man matures, he's able to view sex in a healthy perspective. At that point in a man's life, he knows that sex isn't a sport and women aren't play toys. Men who are mature about relationships and sex have learned from their past experiences and are ready to have healthy and whole relationships. However, *don't assume that maturity about sex and sexual issues comes with age.* Contrary to popular belief, wisdom does not automatically come with age. This isn't a development that occurs just because a man turns thirty, forty or even fifty! Such spiritual maturity comes only when a man is learning from the lessons of life as they are presented to him. Then, and only then, does wisdom come with age. Some men never seem to get beyond the belief that their entire relationship with women is about sex no matter what their age may be.

Last, there are men with deeply rooted cultural and/or religious convictions that govern their views toward sex. Some of these men may be celibate for years or even make it all the way to marriage. Contrary to the stereotype, they aren't all undesirable, weird or effeminate men. One such example is a good friend of mine. He's a handsome, highly educated man who stands well over six feet and drives a sports car—not a nerd in any sense of the word. In fact, looking at him, one would assume he could have as much sex as he possibly desired. But though he could have, he didn't have sex for the first time until he married in his midtwenties because he remained celibate for religious reasons.

Another example of a man who is celibate is Darryl. He describes himself as "functionally celibate." He says as a single father with custody of two kids, he doesn't have time for casual sexual relationships. He feels that such casual sexual trysts would detract more from his life than they would add to it. Therefore he's decided to have sex only within a long-term committed relationship. Since he doesn't see himself doing that any time soon, he's celibate.

When it comes to sex, men fall into three categories:

The sex fiend

This is the man whose every thought about women relates to sex. He's the kind of guy who is constantly sizing up women based upon their sexual appeal. When he sees a woman on the street who appeals to him, he wonders what it's like to have sex with her. He watches television and imagines sex with the women he sees on the television. He is constantly searching for opportunities to seduce women. This man finds himself in constant pursuit of sexual encounters and has little or no self-control when he has a sexual opportunity.

The play-by-the-rules man

This is the man who has graduated beyond the mentality of the sex fiend. While he too has sex on the brain much of the time, he has enough sense to keep it in perspective. While like the sex fiend he's tempted to have no sexual boundaries, he realizes the consequences of womanizing or cheating and weighs them as not being worth the risk. But don't applaud too heartily for him because he's by no means a saint. When single, he's apt to womanize. He just isn't reckless about it. When married or committed, he's the kind of man who will be faithful because of the rules, not because of his heart. If he gets an opportunity for sex outside his relationship that he feels he can get away with, he may take advantage of it.

The higher-thinking man

This is the man who, like the play-by-the-rules man, has an understanding about the consequences of reckless sexual behavior. However, his reason for keeping himself in check isn't because he won't break the rules. It's because he sees the higher cause and effect of promiscuous behavior as it relates to himself and others. Where the play-by-the-rules man would take advantage of a situation in which he could get away with it, the higher-thinking man would turn away from the situation on the basis that it didn't serve the ultimate good of his relationship. If he's single, he may not see it as a wise choice for his own personal integrity. An analogy would be speeding while driving. A play-by-the-rules man would follow the speed limit so he wouldn't get a ticket. When he thought no cops were around, he'd speed. Conversely, a higher-thinking man would follow the speed limit because he realized speeding endangers lives. Most hidden lovers are typically in the latter category.

> **IMPORTANT NOTE:** These aren't categories with rigid boundaries. Depending upon the circumstances in his life at the time, a man could find himself vacillating among these categories.

An entire book could easily be devoted to the subject of what men think about sex. This chapter mentioned the distinctions in the male views of sex only as background for better understanding the hidden lover's views on sex. Now that I've defined how the hidden lover (typically the higher-thinking man) views sex, let's listen to what these guys have to say about sex.

SIX THINGS HIDDEN LOVERS WANT TO SHARE WITH WOMEN ABOUT SEX

Hidden lovers don't want to have sex all the time.

"Honestly, sometimes I just don't feel like having sex. Especially if I'm tired or I have to get up early the next morning. Sometimes I just want to lie there and chill."—Chris, 28, paramedic

Believe it or not, all men aren't salivating dogs when it comes to sex. Chris, a robust paramedic, told me about a situation in which he didn't feel like going home because he knew his girlfriend was going to come by to see him that night and she'd want to have sex. He said there were some occasions when he would rather just hug and snuggle and save the hot sex for a time when he could put the energy and time into it to make it good. To some this story may be funny because it sounds like such a role reversal. But as previously stated, the hidden lover loves sex as much as anyone, but it doesn't dominate his better judgment. There are times when Chris feels it would be better to relax and enjoy his girlfriend's company than to have sex. Of course, he wasn't the only hidden lover who expressed this feeling of feeling pressured for sex. Though they want their wives/girlfriends to know this, many of the hidden lovers I spoke with admitted they have not expressed it, or haven't expressed it emphatically due to fears of being seen as not manly enough to satisfy their woman.

For some hidden lovers, sex feels like a duty.

"My wife and I have a certain method we follow in order to help us both become aroused and climax. But it makes me feel like a love slave sometimes because she's giving directions and commands."—Richard, 37, insurance sales

Richard said his wife is like a drill sergeant, telling him exactly how to move, what position to get into and coaching him through the session until she climaxes. He said he even got a cramp once but didn't dare to move from the position until she had an orgasm. He admits that overall he enjoys sex with

Stopping the glitch.

his wife, but he secretly wishes it felt less dutiful. When asked what could be different, Richard says there's no spontaneity to provide the spark of excitement. He said he'd like to just break their routine to see what would happen. But his secret fear is that if his wife doesn't enjoy the change of routine she'll be angry with him. So he just continues to serve in silence.

What happens outside the bedroom affects things in the bedroom.

"If I have a great day at work and I feel like I'm the man, I'm good to go for some serious lovemaking with my wife. But when I have a bad day, especially a string of bad days at work, I don't even have strength to think about sex. I also don't even feel attractive on those days."—Jonathan, 25, educator

Jonathan summed up how many hidden lovers feel about the way the outside world, especially their careers, affects their sex drive. Another man put it bluntly, "When I'm doing well in business, I can get it up more easily." For hidden lovers, sexual feelings can be closely tied to our sense of accomplishment. If we're feeling successful, we feel more sexy. If we've just suffered a defeat, we feel lower in self-esteem and even unable to perform. Of course sometimes our wives/girlfriends can help pull us out of these quagmires with their feminine wiles, but not always. It's important when your best seduction-and-soothing efforts don't seem to help, not to take it personally. He'll snap out of it in due time. You haven't failed him just because you couldn't get his mind off things. Time might be better spent together in other ways.

Hidden lovers want their women to be sexually aware of themselves.

"My wife said she wanted to have a really big orgasm. At first I felt like she was saying I wasn't good in bed. But after she explained what she meant, I understood that she was saying she didn't know if she was getting all she could from her orgasms so we went to the bookstore and got a couple of books on the subject. Then we did research!"—Kevin, 32, technology professional

The hidden lover wants his woman to be sexually satisfied. He wants her to have an immensely satisfying sexual experience with him. But some hidden lovers secretly complain that their wives/girlfriends don't take enough responsibility for their own sexual fulfillment. As one man stated about his wife of several years, "She just doesn't know how to get off real good!" When a woman doesn't understand her own sexual response and stimulation, it places a great deal of pressure on the man to satisfy her. In contrast, women who are aware of their sexual response and stimulation can work together with their mate during sex for a mutually satisfying result.

Technical difficulties

"For a couple of months, I'd been having trouble getting an erection. I was too embarrassed to even try to have sex with my wife. I felt like crap. She was understanding but I know she was just as frustrated as I was. I went to the doctor and found out my condition was treatable."—Victor, 46, accountant

Hidden lovers and other men are all subject to technical difficulties with their erections. The scientific name for these technical difficulties is impotence, described as "the total inability to achieve erection, an inconsistent ability to do so, or a tendency to sustain only brief erections." It is believed that impotence affects 10 to 15 million American men.

If you are affected, there is no reason to panic and it's not the end of the world! Impotence is treatable. Often it has a physical cause such as disease, injury or drug side effects. Experts estimate that 10 to 20 percent of impotence cases derive from psychological factors including stress, anxiety, guilt, depression, low self-esteem and fear of sexual failure.* These factors are also often present in cases of physical impotence and brought on by the physical issues. So tell your man not to panic if he's experiencing technical difficulties. He's not alone. Just get some help.

*Statistics and information derived from the National Institutes of Health, National Kidney and Urologic Disease Information Clearinghouse website, 2002.

Does size matter?

"I'm afraid that I'm too small to satisfy a woman."—Ricky, 22, college student

Judging from the number of men who've brought up similar concerns at my website, I feel it's important to address this point for hidden lovers as well.

To understand this situation, we have to go back to childhood. A little boy is curious about his penis. At a very early age he wonders if his is normal. That's one of the reasons little boys engage in the ancient bathroom game of urinating together. I suppose it's some sort of boyhood bonding ritual and one purpose it may serve is to give us a chance to see another boy's hardware in a nonthreatening way, thus reassuring ourselves that we're normal.

But even as grown men, wondering about the adequacy of our penis doesn't cease. Men who know for a fact that they have a large penis feel secure on the size issue. Men who are smaller sized, or don't know whether they are "sizing up" (pun intended), tend to feel insecure on the issue. Ask women formally and most will say size doesn't matter. But in small circles they giggle about the size of some men and exchange stories. I remember a woman once telling a story about a big buff guy she was dating. One night they were about to have sex for the first time and, upon seeing his small penis, she was shocked. She says she stopped the foreplay right then and there and accidently let a giggle slip out. Not only did he need a cold shower, I'm sure he needed a cure for a bruised ego too.

Penis size is a matter of preference. Some women prefer thickness, some prefer length, some both! It's all subjective. Yet the stereotypes persist that a man with a large stiff penis is truly a man, a real lover, and as long as that idea is alive and well, men will continue to wonder about their own penis and rate their self-esteem accordingly.

THINGS TO THINK ABOUT

1. How's your sex life? Does your man share the same opinion about your sex life as you?
2. Do you feel sexual pressure in your relationship?
3. If you're single, have you considered celibacy? If so, what role does it/will it play in your dating life?
5. Do you feel there are complications caused by sex outside of a commitment? What are those complications?
6. How do you think men see sex differently than women? How do they see it similarly?
7. How are the changing roles of women in today's society impacting the way women view sex and relationships?

JOURNAL EXERCISE

What are your feelings about sharing your body sexually with a man? Under what circumstances do you prefer to be sexually involved? Compare this to situations in which you've actually been sexually involved. How do you approach sexual involvement in your life? Do you envision that changing or remaining the same? Why?

LETTER FROM THE HIDDEN LOVER, PART 8

For a while I was afraid there might have been something wrong with me. It wasn't that I'd lost my interest in sex, that wasn't the case at all. But I found myself not always wanting sex or thinking about it every moment of the day the way I did when we first became a couple. I'm sure you noticed because I wasn't always wanting it the way I did before. But that's because something changed after we became a couple and I was afraid that you weren't going to understand my new view on sex in our relationship.

To convince myself that there was nothing wrong with me I had to analyze what was different about sex now versus when we were dating. When we were single, two footloose and fancy-free spirits just hooking up when it was convenient, that was a different world than the one we live in now. Now we experience all of our lives together, every phase. Now we're together when one of us has had a bad day, or when one of us is tired and stressed. So instead of seeing each other only when "it's time," we see each other all the time. Therefore, we have to work at creating times, the right times, for romance.

According to the myth, guys are supposed to be obsessively horny and always ready. I know that's what you see on the beer commercials and in movies. Guys wanting sex all the time. Guys thinking about sex all the time. In fact, that's what made me think something was wrong with me. But after we'd been married awhile, it was as though I wanted to add more to my sexual relationship with you—more than just my body. Oddly, that's how I knew I really cared for you—because my thoughts about you weren't only sexual. And that's when a man knows a woman has his heart—when he feels for her so deeply that he can think of her as more than a sexual object. But please understand, that's no indictment of you. You're very sexy. I am happy to say that instead of fantasizing about women I see on television, I fantasize about you.

I've found that as I've entered a new phase in my life as a married man that my love for you is expressed sometimes in ways other than sex. Going to work every day is expressing my love for you. Washing your car every weekend is expressing my love for you. Working at being a good man is expressing my love for you. Of course, I greatly enjoy showing you how I feel in bed much more than washing your car! But you get the point.

When I see these magazines saying how many times the average couple has sex I always wonder whom they're polling. Is it college kids, the wild single bunch, or people who've been married ten years? Each group would give a different answer because their understanding of love and intimacy is in a different place, as are their duties and priorities. I mean, in real life, stuff comes up and you can't do it on a schedule like sex is sandwich night or something. And believe it or not, that doesn't bother me. Sometimes I enjoy just cuddling with you and watching a movie. I'd rather wait to make quality love to you than do a quickie. Unless of course we're both in need of maintenance, in which case a quickie will do.

Then there's the quality-of-sex issue that I sometimes worry about. As a guy, I'm always concerned about whether I'm really satisfying you. I know you say I do. But if you don't have an orgasm when we make love I really feel bad. At those times I get concerned that I'm not satisfying you and I get really self-conscious. I know it doesn't happen much but when it does I feel bad. Then there are times when I haven't gotten off though you might have thought I did. It doesn't happen much but it has on occasion. I guess it just goes to show that there's more to sex for a man who is in love than just his body.

I guess what I'm saying in all of this rambling on about sex is that I love you and I also love making love to you. Being married has taught me that there's more to satisfying my woman than sex. It has to do with our entire life together. I don't just want to make love to you in bed; I want my entire life to be a way of showing my love for you. I hope this doesn't sound too wimpy. But it's how I feel.

CHAPTER 9

WHY THE HIDDEN LOVER FEELS HE CAN'T REALLY TALK TO YOU

The scene is all too common; a couple sitting on opposite ends of the couch after an argument. Maybe they're staring at a television set, not really watching. Perhaps one of them has stormed out in frustration. Both of them are probably wondering why the other person can't see whatever the issue is their way. To each of them it all seems so clear from his or her side that the other person just isn't being logical. Truth be told, I can be one of those guys who has no idea what his wife means sometimes; and at those times it takes a sincere effort to understand.

In the comments section of a survey on my website, I invited people to share what they felt was the most important thing a couple could do to bring out the best in their relationship. Virtually unanimously the comments by both men and women emphasized communication as the number-one issue in a relationship. But then, why don't we communicate? Furthermore, why don't we understand each other when we do talk?

Talking is simple when the subject matter is easy or when both people are in a good mood. But communication is the first thing to go out the window in a tough situation. This is usually when hidden lovers close off. Why? This chapter explains and demonstrates some of the reasons men shut down instead of communicating. The examples below aren't intended to make it sound as though the man is right in each situation. Rather, they're meant to give women a window into our thoughts. Read each example in this chapter and you'll get a view from the male side of the fence on what we're hearing and feeling. Let's look at some examples of why hidden lovers say they can't talk to women. Please note as you read these examples that they are strongly dramatized in order to make their points more obvious.

THE MIND READER

The woman who plays this role doesn't listen objectively to what a man says. Instead, she listens without taking his words to heart. *The mind reader thinks she knows a man's feelings better than he knows them himself.* The problem with mind readers is that they aren't reading a man's mind; they're really imagining what they want him to feel or what they think he feels. Unfortunately, doing so usually only makes things worse. Here's an example of a woman playing the role of mind reader.

Jeannie and Arthur are college seniors approaching graduation day. They've been having problems deciding whether they are going to get engaged after graduation or break up and go their separate ways. Arthur feels that Jeannie is pushing the idea of a strong commitment too soon. Jeannie feels that Arthur is a man who wants to make a commitment but needs his woman to make him aware of the fact. Let's be a fly on the wall as they talk in Jeannie's dorm room.

JEANNIE: Arthur, it's time for us to make a decision. We've come to that place all couples come to at which we need to make a real go of it or go our separate ways.

ARTHUR: Why does everything have to be so serious all of a sudden?

JEANNIE: You know it's true. I know you feel the same way.

ARTHUR: Why can't we just stay the way we are? I'm happy and you're happy. Why do we have to get formal with titles like Mr. and Mrs. and all that stuff?

JEANNIE: I'm not looking for a title. I just want to be engaged at the very least, something more than just dating steadily forever and ever.

ARTHUR (sighing): I really love you. But I have a problem with getting engaged right now. I'm just not feeling I should do that before I find a job and get settled. I don't know if I can make a long-term commitment yet because I don't know what I'll be doing six months from now. I need to get established so I'll have something to really offer you in a life with me. I don't want to look up six months from now and we're living in a dive somewhere while we go around trying to get any job we can find. You know what I mean?

JEANNIE (crossing her arms and looking analytical): This is really about you thinking that we don't have what it takes as a couple to pull together and overcome difficult situations. You don't have the faith in us that I do. You don't think we can do it, but we can. I've already talked to my company and they're going to allow the summer interns first opportunities in their new management training program. I'm going to have a good job. I've also thought about what you could do to make yourself know we can make it. With your grades and résumé, you could easily get a good position here instead of moving back to Chicago. There are plenty of banks here that would hire someone with your résumé. We can always move back to Chicago later.

ARTHUR: You're not getting it. You just don't understand how important it is to a man to be able to
have a stable career before he settles down, or at
least be started on a career track. Right now I
don't know which way I'm going after graduation. I
can't add a new engagement to all of this right
now. It's too much pressure.

JEANNIE: I hear everything you're saying. But what
you're really thinking is that you're afraid to trust
in our relationship.

THE DICTATOR

The woman who plays the role of dictator is impossible to talk
to. The dictator woman will allow a man to say only what she
feels is appropriate. *The dictator woman will tune out of a discussion if she feels her mate is saying anything she doesn't
want to hear.*

Kelly and Jeff, a married couple, are in the midst of a
heated argument. Kelly is angry that Jeff was late paying a
credit card bill and the company has now charged a substan-
tial late fee and raised their interest rate.

KELLY: I thought you said you paid all the bills last
month.

JEFF: I thought I did too. I guess I missed that one.

KELLY: Well, your mistake is going to cost us and we

don't have money to waste like that. Not to mention our credit rating. How are we ever going to qualify for a mortgage if we don't pay our credit cards on time?

JEFF: Oh, excuse me, Ms Financial Genius. I guess you've forgotten about the time you forgot to pay the electric bill!

KELLY: That was before we were trying to qualify for a home loan. Don't try to change the subject.

JEFF: I'm not changing the subject, I think this is very relevant. The fact is we both make mistakes. But why is it that when I make a mistake you jump all over me and when you make a mistake you don't want to talk about it? That's something that really bothers me and I want to discuss it!

KELLY (angrily): I don't want to talk about this anymore. This conversation is over!

IGNORANCE IS BLISS

Similar to the mind reader, the ignorance-is-bliss woman doesn't really listen to the man; instead she hears only what she wants to hear. This woman's motto is "see-no-evil, hear-no-evil, speak-no evil." *The ignorance-is-bliss woman glosses over anything her mate may say that could be upsetting for him, her or the relationship.* She's difficult for her man to talk to because he can never really get any useful feedback from her. She's so concerned about not rocking the boat that she considers it taboo to offer any advice or opinions.

Ed and Rhonda have been married for twenty-three years. During that time, Rhonda has been a housewife and stay-at-home mom. Ed is a construction supervisor, a demanding position that places him between irate construction workers, his nervous boss and their demanding clients. Often he would like to bounce ideas off his wife about how to deal with difficult people at work, but he doesn't get any help from her in that area.

Let's observe Ed and Rhonda sitting at the breakfast table.

RHONDA: You hardly ate any of your breakfast. Do
    you feel okay?
ED: I'm just not looking forward to this meeting. The
    boss wants to fire a guy because he's been late
    twice this month. But he's one of my best workers
    and he's been with me for five years. The poor
    guy's wife is on disability and he has two kids. If
    he gets fired he could lose his home. I've been
    fighting for him but nobody else is helping me.
    Today they're calling us all in for a meeting. I
    know they're going to fire him right then and there.
    [Ed puts his face in his hands and rubs his face
    while letting out a groan.]

RHONDA (taking Ed's plate and patting him on the
    back with the other hand): Everything will be all
    right, honey. What do you want for dinner?

Ed rolls his eyes and shakes his head at the ceiling.

THE INTERPRETER

One of the most common and most difficult women for a man
to talk to is the interpreter. She's very similar to the mind reader except she doesn't claim to have the supernatural power to
understand what a man thinks. *The Interpreter believes she can
say what a man thinks better than he can say it himself.*
Whereas the mind reader simply believes she knows a man's
every thought, women who are interpreters run everything a
man says through their "feminine filter." Whatever he says,
she restates the way she believes he meant to say it.

I actually had this happen on a television show as I was
explaining this very point. I was taping an episode of the *Men
Are from Mars, Women Are from Venus* show, explaining to
the audience how women tend to reinterpret what men say.
No sooner had I finished than a woman on the panel jumped
in and began to restate what I'd just said. I laughed and
looked at the audience, saying, "You see! This is a case in
point."

Here's another example. David and Susan are confronting
a classic issue for couples. David is feeling the need to get
away and feel independent, a need so many of us men cher-
ish having fulfilled. But Susan isn't understanding this as
David attempts to explain it to her.

DAVID: Susan, I love you and I love being with you.
But for the two years we've been married, I feel like
I haven't had much time to myself. I have an urge
to go out and do something alone. It would do me a
lot of good.

SUSAN: What you're saying is that you're feeling like
I'm holding you hostage.

DAVID: No, actually I'm just saying that I'd like to
drive down to Atlanta to see my brother and I'd
like to go alone.

SUSAN: What you're saying is you feel that I'm keeping you from having a life of your own.

DAVID: Not really. I told you I love spending time
with you. But a man needs to feel independent
sometimes.

SUSAN: So what you're saying is this marriage is a
burden to you all of a sudden.

DAVID: Could you just listen instead of trying to tell
me what I'm saying?

THE MANAGER

This is probably the most frustrating of all conversationalists. The manager is quite similar to the interpreter and mind reader, only a more severe case of both. *The woman who plays manager tries to actually supervise and manipulate a man's feelings instead of listening to how he says he feels.*

Let's take Nancy and Chris, for example. Since the time they've been engaged, they've had more trouble than they've ever had in their year and a half together. Lately, it seems that most of their time together is spent arguing about details of the big wedding they're planning. Their scene begins as they stand in the church with their wedding consultant planning the details of the ceremony.

CHRIS: I think we should have the groomsmen stand over here for this part.

NANCY: No! Chris, you don't want to do that. It doesn't make sense.

WEDDING CONSULTANT: Actually, he does have a point.

NANCY: No. No. No. He's just forgotten that we've already talked about all of this.

CHRIS: We didn't talk specifically about this part. Don't forget this is my wedding too. I like my idea and even the consultant agrees.

NANCY: I think you're just getting tired and
   grumpy.
CHRIS: I'm not tired and grumpy. I just want to have
   some input into my own wedding ceremony.
NANCY: Chris, you're making a bigger deal over this
   than I think you realize. It's not really a big deal
   if the groomsmen stand where I suggested. You'll
   like the way it looks. I know what I'm talking
   about.

THE FLAME THROWER

As her name implies, the flame thrower is a dangerous
woman to try to have a conversation with. *The flame thrower
has her guard up and can't have a conversation without taking something personally and launching into an argument.*

   Dan and his girlfriend Sheila enjoy going out to dinner on
the weekend. They love fine food, maybe a little too much.
Both have been steadily gaining weight and neither has
worked out in ages. Realizing this, Dan decided to get them
a membership at a new local gym. But first he had to give
Sheila a hint that they needed to lose weight. Knowing her
temper he knew to tread lightly.

DAN: I have a couple of free passes to the new gym
   down the street. Let's check it out. If we like it we

can get a discount on membership by joining together.

SHEILA: I don't want to go.

DAN: Come on, it'll be fun. We can sweat off some stress and get these bodies buff.

SHEILA (standing defensively with her hands on her hips): What are you saying? Are you saying I look fat. I'm not fat!

DAN: No, you're not fat. I was just hoping that we could join together so we could both tighten up some and lose a few pounds in the process. We've both put on a little weight lately. If we start working it off now it won't become a big problem later.

SHEILA (rocking her head and working her neck): Look, when we started dating I told you I was going to be myself and I wanted a man who would love me for who I am. I have natural curves in all the right places. I will never look like those sickly pencil-thin models in fashion magazines. Half of them are starving themselves to death to look like that. I read an article in *People* the other day about women in Hollywood who were starving themselves to look thin. I'm not going there. If you want somebody who looks like that you can take your butt right down there to the gym and take your pick. I'll find somebody else. Somebody who appreciates the beauty of my natural curves!

DAN: I didn't say anything about being as thin as a
   pencil, I'm just saying we both need to lose weight.
SHEILA (exploding): Maybe you just need to get yourself a new girlfriend!

MEN WANT TWO SIMPLE THINGS FROM CONVERSATIONS

In the previous dialogues men were shown being frustrated with attempts to communicate with their mates. In all of the situations, the men felt they were being denied two things that are crucial to men being able to feel satisfied with a conversation:

1. *We want to know that what we say is being* HEARD. Simply listening to what a man has to say allows him to feel that his opinion matters and that he is being respected for what he has to say.
2. *We want to know that what we are saying is being* VALUED. Valuing what a man has to say doesn't mean you agree with everything he has to say. However, it does mean that you acknowledge the validity of what he has to say.

Much of the time when men flare up in a conversation and it degrades into an argument, it's not so much about whether they feel they are losing an argument, or wrong or right. Much of the time it's about whether they feel they're being listened to and valued for their opinion. If those two needs are met, a man will be much easier to talk to, even when the subject is something unpleasant to him.

THINGS TO THINK ABOUT

1. On a scale of 1 to 10 (ten being the best), how would you rate yourself on listening to your man?
2. On a scale of 1 to 10, how would you rate the way you talk to your man, particularly in debate or argument situations?
3. Do the types of poor listeners in this chapter tend to be mostly women or have you known both men and women to have the conversation styles shown in this chapter?

JOURNAL ENTRY

Think of a time that you had something really important to say to your man. How did you say what you had to say? What effect did it have on him? Would you communicate your message the same way today?

Also, think of a time in your relationship that he told you something important pertaining to the relationship. Was he tactful? Compassionate? Cold? Reflect on how what he said made you feel. Could something have been stated differently?

A LETTER FROM A HIDDEN LOVER, PART 9

We have an obstacle blocking our ability to communicate as well as we could as a couple. Sometimes, I don't feel you and I really talk to each other as much as we talk at each other. I'm open to you telling me what I can do to communicate better with you. But in this letter I'm going to tell you what you can do to communicate better with me.

I know you already understand that I have trouble expressing my feelings with words and to help me you often put things into words for me. Sometimes when I'm staring at the wall trying to get out exactly what I want to tell you, you'll say, "What you're trying to say is . . ." Most of the time I don't really mind when you do that.

But I mind when you reinterpret my words when we're having a heated debate or even an argument. If we're arguing, debating or having a heated discussion—however you want to put it—you have a tendency to go into this mode of thinking in which you take everything I say and reinterpret it. This is a big obstacle to our communication because you're trying to think of what I should be saying or thinking instead of listening to what I have to say. Then we go round and round with me saying something and you turning it around in your mind and telling me what you think I'm trying to say. Or you will jump ahead and start arguing with me based upon what you thought I meant. That's when it almost gets funny because at that point you're not arguing with me directly, you're arguing with what you thought I meant or what you think I'm going to say!

Getting back to the point of this letter, when I say we have a couple of communication obstacles, I'm not saying we don't talk because we talk a lot. In fact we always say we can talk to each other about anything. But I have to admit that when I say that I have some stipulations. I mean I don't really feel that I can talk to you about any and every thing.

There are some things that I would rather keep to myself or bounce off a male friend. Sometimes you get offended when I tell you that I don't think you'd understand something I'm feeling because you're a woman. You think I'm saying that as an insult. But I don't mean it as an insult—it's a fact. There are some things men feel better about relating to other men about. By the same token, there are things I'd never discuss with the guys that I feel I can talk only to you about. As a man who's trying to get over being a hidden lover, I'm trying to learn to open up to you more and stop hiding the intimate part of me that you are entitled to as the woman in my life. But that doesn't mean I won't have some privacy. There's a fine line between having personal thoughts and feelings and being a hidden lover, and I'm learning where that line is drawn. Yes, I am too hidden right now. But even after I get beyond being a hidden lover, I will still reserve a private part of myself. Doesn't everybody?

THE LADIES HAVE THEIR SAY

Things Women Want Their
Hidden Lovers to Know

Throughout this book, I've been discussing the various things that hidden lovers want their wives or girlfriends to know, but have difficulty telling them or getting them to understand. Many of those things have been revealing, albeit somewhat uncomfortable or politically incorrect. Yet, in the spirit of healing the gender gap, they needed to be stated. But what about the other side of the equation? Surely, women have some things they wish their hidden lovers knew, but have difficulty telling them or getting them to understand. In this chapter, I've turned the tables and let women have their say. The information for this chapter was gathered from a survey conducted from my website and comments from audiences at my discussion forums.

Why I feel it is so important for you to talk to me.

In a relationship, communication is extremely important; but the sexes communicate differently. Women tend to be more verbally expressive than men. For this reason, women often want to thoroughly discuss things affecting a relationship. On the other hand, men can easily feel annoyed by the very idea of too much discussion about an issue. Add to this the fact that hidden lovers aren't comfortable discussing emotions and feelings anyway, and you have the makings of yet another situation in which a woman will want to talk and the man shuts down.

Women who've responded to my questionnaires have indicated that shutting down is one of the most difficult things for them to endure in a relationship. They want their hidden lovers to know that when a man shuts down it leaves his significant other feeling as though she's been shut out of an important part of his life, particularly as it relates to the health of their relationship. Women want hidden lovers to know that talking things out in a relationship is critical to their feeling safe and secure and that thus it is one of the most important improvements a hidden lover can make in a relationship.

Let me know how I can help you.

Closely related to the issue of talking and communicating is the desire that wives and girlfriends have to help their hidden lovers. Wives and girlfriends of hidden lovers want them to know that they are ready, willing and able to help their men through the issues they are facing that block their ability to heal emotional wounds and open themselves up to their relationships fully. Many of the women from whom I have received responses not only feel that helping their hidden lovers through difficult situations is important, they also feel it is a responsibility that comes with the relationship. But they want men to know that they can't help with problems men won't reveal.

What have I said or done that has hurt you?

Sometimes a hidden lover may harbor resentment for things his wife or girlfriend has said to him in the past. She may or may not be aware of it, yet it continues to pose a problem as he continues to hide his resentment. Instead of saying what bothers him, the hidden lover will often reveal his frustrations and problems through his behavior—which becomes a woman's clue that something is wrong. However, what women want from men in this situation is a direct statement of the problem. When a man feels he's been mistreated only a direct statement to his significant other about how he feels will work in bringing the issue to the surface and resolving it.

I want to feel closer to you, but your resistance to opening up keeps me from opening myself up more.

A man can't expect a woman to carry all of the emotional issues in a relationship. He has to participate emotionally as well. Women want hidden lovers to know there is a limit to how much they can feel safe and secure in a relationship when he has hidden issues and feelings that are actively affecting the relationship. Though this does not usually altogether keep a woman from loving a man, it is a hindrance that places obstacles in the path of any couple that wants to grow together and become more intimate.

I have some hidden lover issues of my own.

Though this book is about the hidden issues of men, women want their hidden lovers to know that many of them have their own issues to deal with as well. Many women live their lives concealing secrets about their past that they feel are too painful to revisit. Some women have issues resulting from difficult childhoods. Other women have formed deep negative impressions of men due to some type of rejection they experienced with their fathers. Finally some women conceal secrets about past abusive relationships or sexual abuse, either of which could have a significant impact on how they feel with men in relationships.

I feel that if you worked on your relationship the way you work on your career, we'd have a better relationship.

Women have noted how men invest themselves, mind, body and soul, in their careers. But while acknowledging the importance of a man's career, women want hidden lovers to put some effort into developing their relationships. They want men to know that if they took only a fraction of the willpower they use at work and applied it to their relationship, they would see great improvement. Asking a man to work at his relationship the way he works at his career isn't the same as being jealous of his career's place in his life. This is an issue of priorities. What women are saying is that they want their men to treat their relationships as a high priority, not as something taken for granted, thinking that problems and issues will somehow go away or just aren't worth being addressed.

Stop making excuses for your problems and do something about them.

Women have heard all of the excuses men use to explain why they were cheating, why they can't be with only one woman for too long, why they're afraid to commit, etc. Some men even create scientific excuses. They point to genetics and theorize that men just can't be monogamous because it's not in their genes. Some point to history, using some ancient tribe or king as evidence of how men should have many women, a harem. Others are more straightforward: they have a "boys will be boys" attitude. Comedian Flip Wilson had his own excuse for acting up; he'd say, "The devil made me do it." That was a comical line, but the excuses men create for their behavior when it comes to lying, cheating or being half (or less) of the man they should be in a relationship are often just as ridiculous.

Men tend to create excuses that satisfy their own minds, but may make little or no sense to the other person involved. Granted, some guys are struggling with issues. But they have to realize that the woman they're involved with may also be dealing with tough issues. Pulling excuses for poor behavior out of the sky and expecting her to be satisfied with them won't solve anything. Facing up to a problem will. Women appreciate a man who can stand up and face the problems in a relationship. Although that doesn't guarantee a woman will see eye to eye with him, she'll respect him for being the kind of man who faces up to a situation instead of making excuses or running from them.

I'm not like your last girlfriend/wife.

Men are bad about this one. Making a commitment is already a big enough bridge to cross for so many men, and when they do, if the relationship doesn't work out, they're crushed. After that, they think every woman in the world is Hurt'em Helen—the woman who broke their heart.

It's not unusual to hear a heartbroken man say he'll never

trust a woman with his feelings again. Of course, that's an overstatement; eventually he does. But he will probably get the shakes every time the new woman in his life—we'll call her Reba-the-rebound-woman—does anything to remotely remind him of Hurt'em Helen. Then he's on the slippery slope of painful old memories. When that happens his old fears start popping up and making trouble for his new relationship. Instead of seeing Reba-the-rebound-woman as an individual, he may see her simply as a "woman." In other words, much like the other "woman" who hurt him. But he will never create a good relationship thinking that way. Every man wants to be treated as an individual, and not as the last guy who broke her heart. The same is true for women.

Don't hold back important things because you think I can't handle it.

Women don't like it when men treat them like vulnerable little lambs—withholding information because they think women can't handle it. This does more harm than good. For example, let's say a couple is facing a financial crisis and the husband is the only one aware of it because he's been the one handling all the couple's financial issues. Why shouldn't he tell his wife? Wouldn't his wife rather know sooner than later that they're in a financial crisis? Yet some men feel they have to handle all of the bad news because they believe that's part of being a man. What it really does is start to eat a hole in his peace of mind. If he's withholding information that should be shared and worked out in common, he's bringing undue stress upon himself that will sooner or later surface in his relationship in some negative way. In the long run, it's better if both people participate fully in both the good and the bad things that happen in a relationship.

See man and woman as a team.

Women sometimes feel alienated in their own relationships, virtually shut out. One example of when this happens is when a man has a critical issue or a problem he is facing but doesn't want to share it with the woman in his life. That makes her feel as though they aren't really working together as a team, which is important to women in a relationship.

In more extreme situations, some men actually do see their wife or girlfriend as an intruder, a person who is a threat to their peace of mind or livelihood. Such a man doesn't see the woman in his life as a part of a team, but as just another thing in his life to be managed or tolerated. He plays an adversarial role with the woman in his life.

Be willing to work through problems.

It seems that our society has become accustomed to being conveniently committed. Like contact lenses and plastic cameras, relationships and marriages sometimes seem to be disposable items that serve a really useful purpose and then get thrown away. Hidden lovers who want to avoid the responsibilities of a relationship aren't willing to work through the various problems that couples face. Instead, when things come to a crossroad, they leave rather than dealing with the issue at hand. Men often get away with this over and over—so much so that many men have grown accustomed to being able to walk out on relationships and start over with another woman quite willing to take the place of the previous one. As a result, there are men who bounce from woman to woman without remorse or recourse. They know if one woman won't accept their "no obligation or limited obligation" relationship terms, another will.

Stop leaving women and trying to beg your way back.

Boy meets girl. Boy leaves girl. Boy tries to beg his way back to girl. It's the famous final scene of so many movies and novels. But it doesn't happen that way only in the movies and fiction; it happens every day in real life. But why? Why do so many guys seem to keep repeating the same old tired cycle?

The reason for this can be found in the old saying "You never know what you've got until it's gone." Often true for the men who pull this stunt. They have a good woman, but then mess things up. Maybe he even left her for someone else only to realize later that the woman he left behind gave him the best relationship he'd ever had. Then the man comes to his senses and wants to be forgiven. In movies there's a happy ending. But in real life, he may just get the door slammed in his face.

Be yourself.

I've seen guys time and time again try to woo women by acting like someone other than themselves. It must be a strategy similar to a peacock strutting its feathers. When a man is attracted to a woman, he strives hard to impress her. I remember back in grade school, if I liked a girl I'd try to impress her by showing off on the playground in front of her, hoping she'd notice. Likewise, as adults, men try to bolster their image by making themselves seem important, rich or powerful. Whatever it takes to get and keep the woman's attention. The problem, of course, in such an approach is that it can't be maintained under scrutiny. If you say you're an attorney, but you're really a paralegal, she'll find out. If you say you work out every day, but actually haven't exercised since high school, eventually the truth will surface. In such scenarios a man often sabotages his own efforts because after the woman he's trying to impress discovers he's been telling her lies, she won't trust anything else he has to say.

Knowing the art of conversation is essential.

Many women express the desire to have more meaningful conversations with their hidden lovers. While some men are well versed in the art of conversation, others seem to be conversationally challenged. One woman told of a guy she really liked but had to stop dating because of his lack of having anything interesting to discuss. "He was really attractive and athletic. But all we ever did was watch television. We never talked. Even when we did, it was boring. He didn't really have much to say other than talking about really juvenile movies and clothes. I had to move on. I couldn't deal with that."

Some men say the problem is really that women want to talk too much. But here, as in most situations, the real answer is not in blame, but in finding a happy medium. A couple has to have more to do than watch movies, eat together and have sex. That's not a relationship. The relationship comes from the bond that forms through communication and expressing intimacy. That would be difficult to accomplish without meaningful conversation.

Remember birthdays and anniversaries.

This is one of the simple things that men can do to affirm to a woman how much she means to him. We remember things that are important to us. When something is a priority, we make sure to be prepared. Birthdays and anniversaries of wives or girlfriends should be among the important things we remember. The greeting card and floral industries won't let us miss Valentine's Day. But they can't help a man remember his woman's birthday or anniversary. That's one he needs to remember. Guys, if you can't remember it, write it down. I recommend you put those dates on every new calendar you buy as soon as you get it.

A LAST WORD ON THINGS WOMEN WANT MEN TO KNOW

The comments about what women want from men in a relationship were virtually unanimous from the women I surveyed. Yet those things seem to be the best-kept secrets in today's relationships. Women say they want to be treated with compassion, respect and dignity. If a man extends those graces to a woman, she will respond with her love, loyalty, respect and passion. Seems simple, and even lots of men will nod their heads in agreement. But why aren't more men doing it? As a man, I can say that generally speaking, in relationships we need to learn more about the needs of our women.

THINGS TO THINK ABOUT

1. What can you add to the list of things women would like to tell men?
2. What are some subjects you feel a man would be hesitant to discuss with his wife/girlfriend? Why?
3. What is the best way to give someone constructive criticism in a relationship?

JOURNAL ENTRY

What is something that you would like to tell the opposite sex, in general? Write an open letter to the men of America letting them know how you feel about a particular issue.

A LETTER FROM THE HIDDEN LOVER, PART 10

Remember the time we went to the lingerie store in the mall and I pointed out that red outfit a mannequin was wearing in the window? I made a couple of hints about how it was really a hot number and it turned me on. I was hoping you'd catch on to my hints. But either you were ignoring my comments or you didn't hear me so I finally just came out and said what was on my mind. I told you that I'd like to see you in that. Then you snapped, "I'm not wearing anything like that! I'm not walking around our bedroom looking like a hooker in a whorehouse!" Although I know it was a little too wild for your tastes, I didn't know you'd be offended. I quickly jumped back into my shell trying to cover my tracks by saying, "I'm only kidding." But that was a lie. Truth is that I did think you'd look sexy in that outfit and I still do. I can't deny that I'd like to see you in that, even if it's just once. But I never have brought it up again because of how angry you were that I'd want you to wear something like that.

That was a time when I found out that you had things you wanted me to know that you hadn't said to me. At the time, I realized that there were limits to what you'd wear in our bedroom. That's something I didn't know before. That's why although I'm writing these letters to you to let you know how I feel about certain things, I want you to know that I also realize there are many things you want me to know and understand about you. I'm sure you have some things you'd just like to tell me straight, but you're afraid that my feelings will be hurt or that I'll get angry and want to argue. I'll admit, there are some things that are tough to hear and even tougher to talk about. But try me, give me a chance to hear your hidden thoughts and feelings.

I often wonder what things you want to say to me that you hold back. For example, what did you want to tell me that day at the lingerie store? There was clearly some nerve that I hit when I brought up the idea of your wearing the outfit in the window because you rarely react the way you did that day. You have snapped at me only a few times like that before and it was about serious things. Since that day I've always wondered about what was behind your being so offended. Was it something I've said or done? Does it have to do with your ex?

But that's just one example. I know there are other things you want to ask me but don't. Or things you may want to give me ideas and opinions on but don't. One thing I know you'd like to tell me is that you think I should learn to see us more as a team instead of feeling as though everything is my responsibility. I know you want to say that because I can tell how frustrated you get when you hear me droning on and on about how I have to do this and that for the family. Then when you volunteer to take some of the load off me, I insist that it is something that I need to do because I'm the man.

For example, there was the time your car needed to go to

the shop. I'd spoken to the mechanic at length over the phone. I had an understanding with him about what he was supposed to do and not supposed to do, so there was really nothing else left to do but drop off the car. Since you leave your office earlier than me, you should've been the one to drop the car off and I could've picked you up. But instead of letting you drop the car off, I insisted on driving the car to the garage myself, which required me to leave work early. Then I spent the drive home complaining to you about how much work I didn't finish. Once again you told me that you could've dropped the car off. When you said that the second time I realized it was true and I'd brought it all on myself.

I also know there's something a lot more serious in your past that you may want to bring up to me and haven't. Something happened to you when you were a young girl involving one of the neighborhood boys. You've never really said it all, just bits and pieces. But it sounds like something that was traumatizing and left you with really bad memories. That much I can tell. So I want you to know that while I am telling you how I feel about various secrets I have as a hidden lover, I know you have them too. And I hope we can help heal each other with compassionate listening and understanding.

CHAPTER 11

HIDDEN RELATIONSHIP
SINKERS

All hidden lovers are holding things in that limit the depth of their relationships, but some of them have an even bigger problem. They're holding things in that threaten to destroy their relationships. Things hidden lovers hold in that could destroy their relationships are hidden relationship sinkers. They quietly sit deep inside growing bigger and threatening to destroy a man and his relationship with the woman who loves him. But what's even more frightening about these hidden relationship sinkers is that they grow inside some men without their significant other being aware of it until the problems surface as unexplained anger, frustration, rage, depression, alcoholism, drug abuse, womanizing, etc. Men are experts at keeping things in and hiding pain. Sometimes they can play the tough role, keeping the chin up, while inside, an emotional issue is eroding their desire for the relationship.

DOES HE VENT OR SIMMER?

When frustrated by something that's bothering him, what does your hidden lover do? Does he become irritable and yell? Or does he hold things inside and pretend they don't bother him?

When it comes to hidden relationship sinkers, there are two types of hidden lovers: those who vent and those who simmer. Though they have a different way of displaying their hidden feelings, both ways result in self-destructive attitudes and negative behaviors which in turn have an effect on the relationship they're in. It's important to note that the two are not mutually exclusive. In other words, a man can be varying degrees of each, or change styles from time to time. Often whether a man is a venter or the type who simmers is related to the issue at hand. Some issues cause men to lose their cool easily. On the other hand, some issues are so deep and painful that men avoid showing reactions to them.

Men who vent

When angry or hurt, venters are men who

    1. Express emotions by raising their voices or yelling.
    2. Throw tantrums.

You don't have to worry a lot about figuring out what the venter is thinking because his actions let you know. Venters can't hold in a lot of extra stress and pressure. When they try, they go off. But getting to the core of the issues of venters can be tricky because once they go into an emotional tirade, venting their anger becomes more important than reasoning.

Here's an example of a venter in action.

Gina doesn't know that her boyfriend Eric is troubled about some things that happened at work. For the past two weeks he's been having serious conflicts with his boss that may lead to him getting fired. Therefore, he's experiencing apprehension about job security and financial stability, two very important components of a man's self-esteem. Needless to say, he's in a bad mood. But because he's the kind of guy who doesn't feel comfortable discussing this with Gina, he goes off on her about something else altogether.

GINA: Hurry up, honey, or we'll miss the first part of the movie again.

ERIC (gruffly): Look, I'm moving as fast as I can. Do you want me to cut my head off while I'm shaving?

GINA: I guess we have a few minutes to spare. I just want to get a good seat this time.

ERIC (exploding): Just go without me! I'm sick of all your nagging!

Now Gina's hurt because Eric has exploded at her for no

apparent reason. This would hurt anyone's feelings. From here the situation could easily deteriorate into a full-blown argument. Sadly, as they argue, unless Eric reveals what he's really upset about, they'll never get to the core of the issue. Eric may even set off some of Gina's issues and then there will be mayhem. In this situation, Eric needs to make amends. He needs to tell Gina what's on his mind instead of going into a tirade.

Men who simmer

When angry or hurt, men who simmer:

1. Avoid discussion of their problems by retreating inside themselves.
2. Find activities to distract themselves from their problems.
3. Deny they have any problems.

It's harder to identify when a man is simmering. This man just avoids dealing with hidden relationship sinkers altogether. Rather than showing at least some sign of internal discomfort, such as the venter's outburst, the simmerer is likely to keep things so deep inside that nobody is able to detect from his attitude the raging issues just beneath the surface. Simmering hidden lovers are often men who don't want to cause trouble or rock the boat. They figure it's best to leave well enough alone. They have a "Why bother" attitude about things. Or they may feel powerless to effect any change and therefore don't even try. That may seem best to them, but it's a situation in which they are fooling only themselves; holding it all in takes a toll mentally, physically and spiritually.

For example, let's look at Ron and Judy. One night Ron had trouble getting and maintaining an erection. The next morning, Judy jokingly mentioned that it might be time for him to ask his doctor for a prescription of Viagra. Though Judy was joking, Ron was deeply affected by the comment. He was already embarrassed about the previous night's performance and hoped Judy wasn't angry about it. Now his feelings were hurt. But being a simmering type, Ron simply mustered a laugh in response to Judy's joke and kissed her good-bye as usual as they both walked to the garage to get their cars and drive to work. During the day, Ron became more deeply affected by Judy's joke. By the time he saw her that evening, he felt sexually inadequate and his confidence had dropped to an all-time low. However, he still hadn't shared any of this with Judy. As a result, Ron was already dreading the next time they would attempt to make love. He feared that again he might not be able to perform satisfactorily. Now, unknown to Judy, her hidden lover has a painful issue building inside him that will eventually affect their relationship. (For more about hidden lovers and sex, refer to Chapter 8, The Hidden Lover's Views on Sex.)

PREVENTING RELATIONSHIP SINKERS

How can women who are involved with hidden lovers help prevent relationship sinkers from taking hold in their relationships? The following are some ideas that can help:

Initiate conversations with him in a subtle way.

As usual, the best thing to do is communicate. The hidden lover needs to listen to the perspective of the woman in his life. Then he needs to articulate his feelings to her. Often talking and getting something off his chest is enough to diffuse a situation. Having open lines of communication also makes it possible for him to feel that he doesn't have to hold things in that keep him from venting or simmering. Let him know he can talk to you. If he doesn't like talking, approach from another angle. Ask him if he will write you a note or send you an e-mail telling you what's on his mind.

Make him feel appreciated.

Once again, the importance of appreciation comes up. Doing little things to make the hidden lover feel appreciated can go a long way in diffusing situations. Men love to have their efforts acknowledged. The way a woman feels special and valued when her husband/boyfriend brings her flowers for no special reason is the same feeling a man gets when his wife/girlfriend takes an interest in his career or compliments him on a job well done (e.g., a household repair or a project for his job). This isn't to say a woman should just flatter a man's ego. Empty compliments won't do any good. He'd probably detect the insincerity and that could actually do more harm than good. Instead, honest heartfelt compliments can erase some of the issues that build inside a hidden lover.

Be attentive to changes in his demeanor.

The best way to address issues the hidden lover has inside is to circumvent the issues before they can take root and grow into significant problems. Wives and girlfriends of hidden lovers can tell when issues are brewing inside a hidden lover by being attentive to changes in habits or attitude. This is because hidden lovers want to have better relationships. Since they do care, when something is bothering them, it will surface in their attitude or their habits. This even applies to the hard-to-read, simmering types. Here are signs that a hidden lover will give that something may be wrong:

1. Though normally witty, he suddenly refrains from saying funny things or laughing at comical things.
2. He changes his ordinary routine, particularly in a way that will postpone his seeing his wife or girlfriend at the usual time.

3. He suddenly becomes dissatisfied with everything
and is constantly complaining.

4. He becomes aloof and detached.

All of the previously mentioned clues are signals that a
hidden lover may be concealing an issue that he's upset
about. By detecting these subtle changes in his demeanor, his
mate may be able to help him open up and work through an
issue before it affects his life or their relationship.

THINGS TO THINK ABOUT

1. What other hidden relationship sinkers can you add to the list?
2. Is your relationship sinking because of one of the issues in this chapter?
3. How can you repair a relationship after the damage caused by a significant problem?
4. Why do relationship sinkers lie undiscovered in relationships for so long?
5. In what ways can a couple work together to detect and eliminate relationship sinkers before they become a big problem?

JOURNAL ENTRY

Write on an issue in your relationship that needs to be resolved to increase communication, intimacy or passion. What are the obstacles to diffusing this hidden issue? Has it become a problem that is snowballing or is it only a small problem at this point? Describe your feelings about the issue and how you can bring it up for conversation.

If you're not presently in a relationship, based on your experience write about how problems in relationships can be diffused before they become threats to the relationship.

A LETTER FROM THE HIDDEN LOVER, PART 11

Do you remember that article from one of those women's magazines last month about the top issues that could break up a couple? We were sitting on the couch and you were reading the article to me. At first I wasn't listening because I thought it was just another one of those articles in a chick magazine. But it was definitely making sense when the writer started listing things that could be hidden relationship destroyers.

One of the things she said really hit home and got me to thinking. It was the part about how hidden resentments of one partner can sink a relationship. That's because for a long time I had some hidden insecurities about your ex. When we got together, he still seemed to be everywhere in your life, although you'd been divorced for over two years. I guess it was because you two had such a nasty divorce that you and I kept feeling repercussions from it. Remember when the house he kept as part of the settlement went into foreclosure and he tried to leave us holding the bag? We had to hire a lawyer to keep us from being held liable for the debt, which cost us two thousand dollars!

Then there was the way he treated you. That caused more resentment in me. And to add to that, I had some hidden resentment toward you for letting him ever treat you that way and allowing him to treat your son that way, too.

The other thing I secretly resented was how my stepson, Nick, looks up to his dad like he's a great father when actually the guy is no good at all. I resent it because I'm the one paying the bills and having to raise him up to be a man while he longs for this fantasy relationship with a father who doesn't care to see him or pay child support. Since the time Nick was two years old, I've really been his father. I guess he'll realize that when he gets a little older. But for now it hurts my feelings every time he starts talking about how great his father is.

Most of this resentment I guess you had some idea of, except for the part about Nick. That's something I guess I'll have to deal with until he's old enough for me to talk to him about it directly. But at five, I don't think he'd really understand. Besides, I'd rather just let him find out on his own that his dad is a jerk so he won't resent me for telling him.

So there you have it. I've had some hidden resentments that at times almost made me wish I'd never gotten married. Most of the time I just suffered in silence although I did blow my top more than once. At least I got to yell directly at your ex a couple of times on the phone, which made me feel a lot better. You and I have talked about most of these things, but only after they had exacted a heavy toll on us, even almost breaking us up once. We've put all that behind us now and things are much better. But that article was right, hidden resentments can be a deadly blow to a marriage or relationship because the problems only grow bigger when left in the dark.

I'm sorry for blaming you about the troubles your ex

brought into our lives. I know that everything I have had hidden resentment about hasn't been your fault. But I have to be honest: somewhere inside of me, I blamed you for all the problems your ex brought and I'm sorry for that. You can't help how much of a problem he's been. I should've talked to you about this a long time ago and the resentment would never have built up inside me.

CHAPTER 12

HELP, I'M IN LOVE WITH A HIDDEN LOVER!

What You Can and Can't Do to Help Him

What can you do to help a hidden lover break free from his emotional bondage? The answer is a tricky one. On one hand, there is a lot you can do. On the other hand, there's actually very little. What I'm leading up to with those intentionally contradictory statements is that a woman has to first be aware of what she can and can't do with a man before she can be of any help to him in changing his life. This involves avoiding two extremes.

The first extreme to avoid is the belief that you are the agent of change in a man's life. I know this goes against all of the romance novels and movies, but it's the truth. When a man really changes, it's because he decided to. That's not to say a woman wasn't around who was part of the influence, but she didn't actually make him change. He changed because he saw more benefit to his life in changing than he did in remaining the same. Yet many women ignore this fact or don't understand it. Too many women seem to feel that it is their duty or some sort of test of their womanhood to change a man. Is it the maternal instinct? In some cases is it neediness disguised as goodwill? Perhaps. But as I've said in every book I've written: Ladies, you can't change a man. He is not a home-repair job that you can redesign and renovate. A woman must remember that she's not the director of a man's transformation, only an actor in the drama.

There's a second extreme to avoid as well. Earlier in this book, I emphasized the damage done to a relationship when a man tries to play superman. (Please see Chapter 4.) This is so important that it bears being reiterated. *Don't let a man play superman in a relationship!* It may be romantic and old-fashioned to some women (and men too). But it's something that can easily lead to a lack of balance and thus one or both people feeling they are being treated unfairly. In terms of the man playing superman, in this role a man feels he is responsible for being the breadwinner, disciplinarian of the children, decision maker, problem solver and super lover. When a man feels that way, it's a formula for hidden anger and ultimately closing himself off in a relationship as his only means of keeping his sanity.

The way to avoid this is by creating a feeling of shared responsibility. A couple should be striving for a sense of equality to avoid either one having to feel like the super partner. This equality doesn't always have to be in terms of money. It extends far beyond that realm into the day-to-day life of a couple. What works as equality for one couple may not be the same for the couple next door. For that reason, it's important for couples to decide what works for them, not look for a hard-and-fast answer. Whatever they do, the bottom line to avoiding the superman mentality is to keep the bearing of responsibilities as even as possible. A man playing the role of superman will almost surely become a hidden lover.

The following are more tips to assist you in helping your hidden lover.

TIPS FOR WOMEN ON DEALING WITH HIDDEN LOVERS

In this section, I've elaborated on some tips for those of you who are in relationships with hidden lovers. For further tips and information on relating to hidden lovers, refer to Group Discussion Topics at the end of the book.

Be your own person.

One of the best tips I can give you about dealing with hidden lovers doesn't even concern the man's behavior. It concerns your approach to life. Women who have a strong sense of self are an asset to a hidden lover in coming out of his shell. This is because women who have a strong sense of self make men feel more comfortable about relaxing. Their men don't feel they have to assume the role of superman. Such women are women with their own opinions, careers, goals and strong character.

Don't allow him to feel like an ATM machine.

It's easy to enjoy it when someone is doing everything for you. In fact, the Prince Charming myth is just that—a handsome rich man sweeps a woman off of her feet and satisfies her every whim. But in reality when a man plays ATM machine, it's destructive to a relationship because he can't continue doing that without developing a feeling that his mate is a dependent, as opposed to being an equal. To keep a man from becoming an ATM machine in a relationship a woman can do things such as earn income or take an assertive role in managing some of the couple's business affairs (i.e., writing out bills, monitoring the budget and expenses, being conscientious about spending, etc.). For unmarried couples, it's good for women and men to share the cost of dating (taking turns paying, splitting the check, etc.).

Don't chase him when he retreats.

The worst thing you can do when a man backs away is to start chasing him. When men back away they're often trying to think or sort things out. Some women, however, interpret this as his backing away from the relationship so they respond by attempting to close up the distance he has put between them. Men feel threatened when this happens and they retreat further. But the further they retreat, the more some women attempt to get closer, and so the cycle continues, pushing him further away. Let him have his space.

Don't overanalyze him.

I've known women who spend hours and hours on the phone with friends trying to analyze every move a man makes. It's good to reflect on things that affect you. But when you're analyzing a man so much that you've gathered enough information to write a textbook on him, you've gone too far. At that point, you're likely to be adding more than is there. You're also only seeing things from one perspective, since you don't know what's making a hidden lover behave the way he is. Last, you've got to remember, you're not a man and therefore will inevitably see things differently; you could be analyzing and interpreting things that he doesn't intend to be communicating to you.

Give him the benefit of the doubt.

The hidden lover is a man who loves his woman but may be having difficulty connecting. Try to see his actions in a less adversarial manner. Work at avoiding the tendency to think he's "acting like a typical man" and then responding defensively based on that. Instead try to see him as an individual. Seek to understand some of his issues and how they have a cause-and-effect impact on him and your relationship with him.

Don't make excuses for poor behavior.

Being understanding and giving a man the benefit of the doubt doesn't mean you're going to let him march all over you and treat you like a doormat. Too many women make excuses for a man's behavior and either live with the false hope that he will somehow miraculously change or just give up and accept behavior that is damaging to themselves. Such an arrangement doesn't help the woman or the man. Making excuses for poor treatment just leads both of them into a worse place.

Try viewing the world from his perspective.

In his important book *Why Men Are the Way They Are*, Dr. Warren Farrell suggests men and women try doing a role reversal so the other person can see things from their partner's perspective. I totally agree. We often spend so much time pointing the finger of blame or feeling that the other person has wronged us that we rarely truly consider the other person's perspective. In doing so, we could learn a lot about why the other person acts the way he or she does. In understanding why people act a certain way we can more clearly see how we could work with them to avoid some of the problems arising in the relationship. The good thing about this approach is that it directly benefits both the man and the woman if they are both willing to do this with an open mind.

Let him heal his own past.

As much as we'd like to, we can't wash away the emotional pain of someone we love. That's just a fact. What we can do is play a supportive role in the healing. We can encourage that person to seek help. We can be understanding and good listeners. But ultimately, the work to make peaceful closure with a painful past is his or her own responsibility. Believing we can repair someone else is a dangerous delusion that sets up a relationship to be out of balance and headed for problems.

Show appreciation for his efforts to change.

When we want people to make a change, it's easy to slip into a critical mode. We will look for what they are doing wrong rather what they are doing right. Case in point was a baseball coach I once had. As catcher, part of my role was to throw out runners who were trying to steal bases. My coach drilled me over and over on throwing the ball to the right spot. When the time came for me to throw out a runner in a game, I was pretty good at it. But to this day, I don't remember him ever saying anything about my pinpoint throws that picked off base stealers. I only remember that he would scream when I didn't make a perfect throw. As a result, I didn't enjoy playing on the team and I'm sure I didn't reach my full potential that season. The same is true in your relationship: remember to spend more time reinforcing the good things the hidden lover does than criticizing. Positive reinforcement is far more effective than criticism.

Seek to understand and to be understood.

Much of this list focuses on how a woman can seek to understand her hidden lover. But this is not a one-sided process. It is important that he seeks to understand you as well. Sometimes we focus on the person needing help without realizing that supporting a person making a change is a tough job too. The hidden lover needs to understand that his actions (or lack of action) can have a detrimental effect on the woman he loves. You need to express your feelings to him so he understands the burden these things are placing on the relationship. This is an important step in his acknowledging responsibility for his actions in a relationship.

Zoom out.

Learn to step back and look at the big picture. Sometimes the answer to what to do is to stop, step back and observe your own life. Listen to what you're saying and feeling. When we zoom out, we sometimes find that we're making a mountain out of a molehill. For example, a woman may be angry that her husband cleaned the kitchen but didn't scrub a couple of pots very well. Meanwhile, the woman next door can't get her husband to help with any of the housework! Sometimes we need perspective. At least the man in the former situation is willingly participating.

Be prepared to see a new man.

If you want a hidden lover to come out of hiding, be prepared for the possibility that a totally different man will emerge. When you invite a man to open up to you, be sure you can handle it. You're inviting him to show you the raw private face of himself that may have been hidden for many years or even all of his life. This could be something you may not be able to handle. You must prepare yourself for this and changes that may come in your relationship with him, because once he tastes the liberation of his new life as a man out of the shell, he won't ever want to go back.

As you think of the information presented in this chapter in terms of your own relationship, remember an important fact. There are rarely, if ever, any hard-and-fast rules that apply to every person in every relationship. It's not my intention for you to read this information and then think it applies to every hidden lover on earth. It's important to consider how the things presented in this chapter apply to your situation. You and your hidden lover may have all of these issues. You may have only a few of them. Or you may have similar but not exactly the same issues presented in this chapter. Avoid cookie-cutter solutions and "rules" for relationships. Take time to look into your relationship and assess what it's going to take for change in your unique situation.

CLOSING THOUGHTS FOR WOMEN WHO WANT TO HELP THEIR HIDDEN LOVERS

In addition to the tips in this chapter, I want to add the following steps for consideration when a woman wants to help her hidden lover.

Don't try to make a woman out of him.

Don't expect a man to think and act as a woman. I get very concerned about some of the dialogues I've heard when a roomful of women starts to analyze male behavior in terms of what *they* think a man should do. They judge him on how *they* feel he should act. If he acted the way they suggested, he'd basically be a man who was acting like a woman. Let's face it—men and women are different. We aren't supposed to think and act the same way. We're complementary opposites, yin and yang, and both absolutely necessary to the other. Part of helping a man change is not trying to feminize him. I'll be the first to say that many men need to be more sensitive. But that's not the same as saying they should be more like women. They don't need to be more like women; they just need to be whole men who are both masculine and sensitive. There's a fine line between those meanings.

Acknowledge your role in the situation.

In any relationship there's an interdependence. It's similar to a dance. The man makes a step, the woman responds, or vice versa. I'm not talking about a co-dependency, but the natural dynamics of a relationship. There's a constant shifting and adjusting. Rarely, if ever, is an issue totally one-sided. How could it be one-sided in a relationship when everything is so delicately balanced between two people? In asking a man to change, it's important to acknowledge what steps you're doing in the dance with him. Otherwise a situation of feeling victimized, blaming and defensiveness can arise and polarize both partners in a relationship.

Here are three important questions a woman should ask

herself when contemplating the changes she believes her man should make:

Can I *really* handle it if he starts expressing his feelings and emotions?

Am I willing to be a co-partner in all phases of the relationship?

Can I be comfortable with him not always taking charge, but instead sharing the decision-making process?

Be patient.

It's important to be patient with a man who's changing. Remember, he's re-creating himself. He's testing out concepts and ideas that he previously may not even have acknowledged as legitimate. It's strange territory and there will be much trial-and-error. Just look at it through his eyes for a moment and realize that this won't be an overnight project. However, it doesn't mean that you should put up with poor behavior from him. Men don't respect women who take all kinds of grief from them and men don't truly love women they don't respect. Be mindful of this during his change process.

THINGS TO THINK ABOUT

1. At what point did you realize you were involved with a hidden lover (i.e., when did you realize your significant other had deeply rooted feelings and thoughts affecting your relationship that he would not share with you)?
2. If you are a hidden lover yourself, can you think of anything that would help you open up? What can your woman do to help?
3. What toll does being a hidden lover take on a relationship?

JOURNAL ENTRY

Take a look at the relationship you're in, or recall a relationship you've had. Write a dialogue between you and that man in which you reveal something to him that you feel is important to the relationship. It can be something you've been holding back that you've wanted to tell him or it could be something about him that you feel you need to discuss. If you recall a particular scene, you could reconstruct it to happen the way you wish it had. Or you could write about the way it actually happened. If this scene hasn't actually taken place you can write what you'd like to have happen. Write about why you chose the events and dialogue you chose.

A LETTER FROM THE HIDDEN LOVER, PART 12

The other day you asked me how you could help me come out of my shell. I wanted to be sarcastic and just say, number one, stop asking me to come out of my shell. But I didn't because that would've hurt your feelings because you were being sincere.

One big thing you can do to help me stop being such a hidden lover is to respect our differences as man and woman. I'm not a woman and I'm not going to think or act like a woman. But sometimes I feel that you want me to see things the way you do and then if I don't you say I'm being a hidden lover. Actually, I'm usually just being a man. I see things differently than you do. When you realize that fact, that alone can have a great positive effect on how we relate.

Of course I'm not saying that everything we disagree on is just because we're of the opposite sex, and I don't want to use that as a cop-out. But please just stick that somewhere in your mind and when you can't see eye to eye with me sometimes, just remember that we're using different vision.

That brings me to my next point. If you'd try to see things from my point of view sometimes, I think you'd have an entirely different feeling about some things I do—some of my opinions and things I may say. I guess what I'm saying is that you should try to walk a mile in my shoes for a day. Then I really think you'd have a better understanding and respect for who I am and what I'm all about. It's kind of like going to work with someone and seeing what they do all day, except with a much more profound impact.

Here's what I suggest. I read it in this book, *Why Men Are the Way They Are*, by Dr. Warren Farrell. He suggests a role reversal. Next time we're having a spat, let's call a time-out, stop and try to see it the other person's way. You tell me all the relevant facts for your side and I'll try to see things your way. Then, I'll tell you all the relevant facts for my side and you try to see it my way. It can't hurt anything and I think it will really help us to have more respect for the other person's opinions.

I know it will help me understand you better because sometimes when I think you're nagging me it's because I really and truly have absolutely no clue why you're so upset. I mean, I may know what the issue you're upset about is, but I don't understand why you're so upset. Then, of course, I just look at you and say, "it's no big deal." Then you get even more upset because you think I don't care. The truth is that I do care, but I just may not realize how important it is to you.

I have another example of how the sexes are different. It's from our vacation last year. After we checked in to the hotel, I brought everything up to the room and just as I was setting the last bag down you said, "I don't want to stay in this room." Then you were on the phone calling the front desk and giving them an earful. You didn't like the fact that we found a couple of hairs in the shower. This is a classic case of male and female differences. I said we should call the maid service and ask them to clean the shower again. But you wanted another room because you didn't feel good about that room anymore. I wanted to fix the problem and stay there because it was close to the pool. But you absolutely couldn't stay there because the thought of those hairs in the shower ruined that room for you. I wasn't happy about moving everything to another room and you weren't happy with my grumbling. You see, we just didn't know where the other person was coming from. That would've been a good time to stop and switch roles.

CHAPTER 13

ANSWERS TO QUESTIONS ABOUT HIDDEN LOVERS

As a follow-up to the previous chapter, I want to address some of the questions women have asked me about hidden lovers. For years now, I've been receiving e-mail and letters in which women have asked me questions about their hidden lovers. Some of the mail is lighthearted and funny. Some of it is serious. Some of it is extremely sad and troubling. It seems the same questions continue to be asked over and over. For this chapter, I reached into my e-mail bag to answer some of those questions directly. These are general answers to specific questions. It's important to remember that you're dealing with an individual in your relationship, not a generalization. Furthermore, I'm not offering therapy here. This book is a book of practical advice, as are the following answers. If you have a specific need, consult a therapist for delving into your issues as a couple or individual. And most of all, do some soul searching. I really believe we have our own answers; we just have to be willing to uncover and accept them.

1. Why is he so afraid I'm trying to trap him in our relationship?

The worst-case scenario for a single man in a relationship is that he will be involved in a relationship that forces him to lose his identity and autonomy. It isn't so much the woman he fears, but rather what he fears may become of him when he gets into a serious relationship with her. He starts having images in his mind of minivans, diapers and a 9-to-5 job with no end in sight. He also fears not being able to hang out with his friends anymore. That's what the fear of being trapped is about; it's about his apprehension that he can't be in a relationship and be himself too. (Please refer to chapter 6, How Fear of Losing Freedom Affects the Hidden Lover.)

2. He says he needs more space. What does that mean?

Men need space, even in a relationship. We go stir-crazy if we think we're being were caged up. To be happy, a man needs a feeling of autonomy. If he feels caged up, or if a woman is holding to him too closely, he'll be apt to put more distance between them, maybe disappear altogether. But if she gives him space, she just may find him opening up more to her. Creating healthy space is something you and your man will have to define in your relationship on your own terms. For some men, it means simply being able to be home alone sometimes. To some men, having space means the ability to go out alone or with friends. Other men define having space as their woman not calling or paging them too frequently. Again, it depends upon the couple. Talk about it and create a workable solution before it becomes a problem.

PLEASE NOTE: I'm not speaking in terms of a man avoiding the responsibilities that come with a relationship. If he can't handle those, he shouldn't be in a relationship. (Please refer to Chapter 6, How Fear of Losing Freedom Affects the Hidden Lover.)

---

3. Why do some hidden lovers start off a relationship red hot and then turn into Mr. Freeze?

He may not necessarily be backing away from you, but he may be starting to feel apprehensive about what you represent in his mind. When some men get to that inevitable crossroad where a relationship has grown as much as it can and it's time to go to the next step or part ways (we all know the place), he turns into Mr. Freeze. Mr. Freeze is a safe place to hide because when a man is playing the Mr. Freeze role he has less to risk emotionally. In his mind, the relationship has become something out of control that is both irresistible and frightening to him. This often brings about other problems. At this point, some women think they can change the man or prove their love to him. But the fact of the matter is that they can't change him and they can never do enough good deeds to prove their love to him because the issues he is dealing with about intimacy are his own project, not hers.

Having said all of that, here are some other points to consider: 1. Was there sex early in the dating? If so, the Mr. Freeze act could be a clue that a woman may have become a member of the flavor-of-the-month club. 2. He may have turned into Mr. Freeze because he was having second thoughts about being in a relationship, or about the woman he was involved with. 3. There's always the possibility that he just wasn't interested in a particular woman and didn't come right out and say it. (Please see Chapter 2, How Hidden Lovers Hide in Relationships.)

4. Is sex a hidden lover's way to feel close to a woman?

Sex isn't the only way for a hidden lover to feel bonded with a woman. The hidden lover is interested in how he relates to his partner as a total woman, not just in the bedroom. Hidden lovers recognize their need for intimacy on several levels and they are men, despite whatever shortcomings they may have, who desire to achieve a high level of intimacy—including sex, but not limited to sex. (Please read Chapter 8, The Hidden Lover's Views on Sex.)

5. How can I help him see where I'm coming from in an argument?

Lay out the facts. "Just the facts, ma'am." Be careful as you lay out the facts that you don't make him feel as though you're already blaming him. Also, don't impose your opinions on him. In other words, be aware that he's coming at the issue from a different perspective, the "male step-by-step blueprint" type of thinking. Don't automatically dismiss his thoughts or feelings as "stupid" or groundless male thinking. If he knows you respect his feelings, he'll be more apt to open up to you. Then you'll be in a much better position to make him receptive to seeing your perspective on the issue. (Please see Chapter 9, Why the Hidden Lover Feels He Can't Really Talk to You.)

6. When I want him to listen to a problem I'm having, he starts lecturing me. Why can't he just listen to me?

Men see things from a problem-solving point of view. If there's a problem, we'd rather just move on it and solve it than discuss it. Whereas women tend to want to discuss things. It's not any better or worse, just different. He may start lecturing you because from his point of view he doesn't understand why you don't just cut to the chase and start looking at solutions to the problem. When you want to tell him something, but don't want him to try to solve it or lecture you, tell him you just want him to listen. (Please read Chapter 12, Help! I'm in Love with a Hidden Lover!)

7. How do I help my hidden lover deal with painful memories from childhood abuse?

That's a serious issue. Abuse, whether sexual, physical or mental, leaves emotional scars that significantly impact a person's life and relationships. He should seek counseling and establish a solid spiritual life. A good therapist could help him recognize, identify and begin the healing process. For creating a spiritual foundation, he should turn to God because on his journey to healing he will need a refuge of strength he feels he can rely upon. (Please read Chapter 3, His Hidden Pain.)

8. What can I do to make him forget about his last bad relationship?

It's a mistake to think you can repair his broken past relationships with something you can do in a present relationship. The truth is that you can't play clean-up-woman for things he's already been through. People on the rebound have to come to terms with their emotional baggage. Until they do, they may be apprehensive, untrusting, oversensitive, suspicious, etc. It's much better to get involved with someone after they've had a good long time to recover from a broken relationship. To try to simply patch over emotional wounds is playing a game of relationship roulette. You can't make him forget about his last bad relationship. And if he's really that worried about it, should he be with another woman so soon?

However, if you're already involved with a man who hasn't recovered from a bad relationship, your situation is different. Navigating such tricky waters will require that you both have patience and compassion. You and your man should seek a good therapist to help guide you through some of the inevitable issues that will arise. But remember, no matter how good your intentions are, you can't repair him. You can only help. (Please see Chapter 3, His Hidden Pain.)

9. Why does he feel he has to take care of me?

Relationships work best when both people have a sense of being treated fairly. However, in American culture, men see themselves as providers and protectors. Though that role has changed and been reinvented, it remains the predominant underpinning to our beliefs. Our society still sees the value of men largely tied to their ability to provide and protect. Therefore, men who feel they can take care of a woman feel they are demonstrating their manhood in one of the best ways possible.

On the outside that may sound like an attractive idea to some women. But in the long run it could lead to resentment on his part. Another thing such a situation could lead to is the feeling that he doesn't have to be accountable to his wife or girlfriend because he pays all the bills and makes all of the major decisions. Or he may feel that she owes him and that's not a good foundation for a relationship. You can't have one person paying all the bills and being responsible for everything and expect to be an equal partner.

Note: Staying home to raise the kids is in fact a job; this person is definitely pulling his or her weight. Hopefully both the man and woman realize that: regardless of who's staying home! (Please read Chapter 5, The Hidden Lover Needs Your Help but Doesn't Want to Ask for It.)

10. Should I let him bear most of the financial burden?

Absolutely not. The answer to this question is similar to the previous one. No matter what a man says, if he's paying all of the bills and having to make all of the major decisions, he can't possibly see her as his equal. Do whatever you can to shoulder at least some of the financial burden of the relationship or household (if it's a couple married or living together). It doesn't matter if he's a banker and you're a waitress, that's okay. Just make sure you contribute a proportion based on your income. Also, as stated above, if you or he stays home to take care of the kids and manage the house, be sure to acknowledge that as a significant contribution to the relationship or family. (Please refer to Chapter 5, The Hidden Lover Needs Your Help but Doesn't Want to Ask for It.)

11. Why does he tell his male friends things that he won't tell me?

With his male friends, he isn't concerned about his thoughts being judged. Nor is he concerned that he will be have to answer questions he feels probe too deeply into his vulnerable spots. With his friends, he naturally feels a safety zone for his thoughts and feelings. That's what friends are for. It's no different than a woman confiding in her girlfriends. Don't feel betrayed or left out. In fact you should encourage him to maintain his close friendships with other men. It's a way for him to feel freedom in the relationship, which ultimately strengthens it and brings him closer to you. (Please read Chapter 9, Why the Hidden Lover Feels He Can't Really Talk to You.)

12. Why can't he open up and share his feelings? After all the time we've been together, doesn't he trust me?

He may trust you, but not be comfortable with his feelings.

Whether you've been together one month or ten years, until he feels comfortable with his own feelings, he can't share them. The important thing is that you don't take it personally. You're not the only woman dealing with this situation. Make it safe for him to open up to you. Give him space and have patience. Expressing feelings isn't something most men have a lot of experience with. In time, he will talk. But don't put high expectations on what he may say. It may be an outpouring or it may be a trickle. (Please see Chapter 1, Real Lover or Hidden Lover.)

13. He says I don't appreciate him. Why does he say that?

When a man says, "You don't appreciate me," what he's really saying is that he doesn't feel loved. It's a man's way of asking for affection. You're not going to hear many men say, "I don't feel loved." Instead, he puts this request for affection in terms of something else. He makes it sound as though you don't appreciate how hard he works, you don't appreciate him cutting the lawn every week, you don't appreciate him for working on your car, etc. But what he really wants is a little tender loving care. (Please read Chapter 7, The Hidden Lover's Need for Appreciation and Respect.)

14. Men complain about women being thin-skinned, but if I were to tell him some of the things on my mind, he couldn't handle it.

That's probably true. Lots of men have really fragile egos that could be crushed without much effort. Then we get defensive. An argument is sure to follow. A suggestion I have for women who want to communicate with men who are difficult to talk to is to preface her comments/complaints with ego-diffusing phrases. For example, when voicing her comment/complaint, she could use statements of fact about how she feels instead of hurling accusations at him. (Please refer to Chapter 12, Help! I'm in Love with a Hidden Lover!)

15. If the hidden lover is a man who wants to be close in a relationship, why do some of them cheat?

When a hidden lover cheats, it actually has less to do with the woman he's cheating on than with his mentality. Such a man obviously isn't cheating because he doesn't have a good partner; it's because something inside him is creating a desire to go outside his relationship. That could be due to a number of things. Often he's struggling with issues that are making him unstable. There are many possible scenarios. But, of course, this isn't an excuse, only an explanation. (Please read Chapter 2, How Hidden Lovers Hide in Relationships.)

THINGS TO THINK ABOUT

1. What other questions do you have about hidden lovers?

2. Have you ever posed these questions to a hidden lover? What was his response?

3. How are your experiences with hidden lovers similar to the issues raised in this chapter? How are they different?

JOURNAL ENTRY

Revisit some of your past experiences with a hidden lover. In retrospect, what things do you now see clearly that you didn't recognize at the time? Hindsight is always easier than foresight, but what have you learned from that experience and how does it affect relationships for you today? Have you recycled that experience into a positive use in your life today? If not, how can you turn that negative experience into something useful for you now?

A LETTER FROM THE HIDDEN LOVER, PART 13

You want answers about how to understand and relate to me? Then ask me, instead of your girlfriends, mother and female relatives! I'm not one of those men who's jealous of his wife's friends or who tries to run off all of your friends. But I do have a problem with the advice some of them have given you.

I'll give you two examples. First, there's Shirley. When we were dating we almost didn't make it past the third date because she had you believing I was a married man out to score. You didn't believe her or you wouldn't have kept seeing me. Still, Shirley believed she was coaching you on how to handle me. But the actual result is that I thought you were kind of weird. Cute, but weird. That was because no matter what I did or said about wanting to date women who were interested in a relationship, you always gave me that look. It was like an interrogation. I remember thinking, "Man, this poor girl must have really been hurt!" But later I learned that look was the result of your listening to Shirley!

Remember how she had you believing that I was married because I had two cell phones? She further supported her case with the fact that I was available only at certain times of the day. As I explained to you that was all a part of my job as a computer systems troubleshooter. But she had you believing it was just an elaborate cover scheme. I also explained to you that one of the phones was paid for by my company and had to be clear all the time in case I was needed on the days I was on call.

Fortunately your actual experiences with me and finding out the kind of man I was won out over Shirley's suspicions. If you'd listened to her, we wouldn't be married today. But just think, if you had asked me instead of listening to her, we could have skipped all that early drama.

The other unrequested adviser you have is your big sister, Anna. I know she's your big sister and you respect her opinion. But she doesn't live with me, sleep with me and eat with me every day, so she can't possibly give you advice on how to deal with me when you need it.

I'm not saying that you don't get valuable advice from other women, because you do. In the same way, wiser men have told me things to make me a better husband. But I'm saying that after you get their advice, you've got to use your own reasoning to apply it to our situation. You've got to look at me for me, not as a "man" doing what supposedly any man would do.

You also have to consider the source. Let's take Shirley, for example. Shirley hasn't been able to stay in a relationship for over a month in the past three years, so how can she give you advice when you've been happily married for three years?

And as for your sister, Anna; she shouldn't be giving anybody advice about men because her husband doesn't even try to get a job. She runs around taking care of him like she's desperate to keep him or something. But then she gets on the phone with you and tells you how you should tell me off about this and that.

Basically, all I'm saying is that when you have a question or a concern about how I'm acting, ask me about it before taking advice from some other woman's world and trying to make it fit our lives. Sometimes their view on things is so different that they can't relate to us. I know I'm not the most talkative person in the world. But at least give me a chance to answer questions about me, or "men," before you ask a woman and then try to apply it to our lives.

CHAPTER 14

WHAT THE HIDDEN LOVER MUST DO TO CHANGE HIMSELF

In Chapter 12, I focused on what a woman can and can't do to help her hidden lover change. To complete that discussion, I now want to turn the focus to what the hidden lover must do in order to change himself. Though I will address these points as what hidden lovers need to do, the information is nonetheless useful to women as a glimpse at the thoughts of the hidden lover. Let's begin by finding out how he feels about his situation and changing it.

The words of a hidden lover: *We were watching this movie last night and the guy in the movie never could tell his girlfriend how he loved her and didn't want to lose her. As I watched I thought about how I'd hate to be in that position because I don't know if I could say the right words either. I do things to show my wife how I feel. But sometimes I know she just wants to hear me say something romantic to her, or something that makes her feel special. I want to but I'm just not good at that! Sometimes I'll think of things to say and then when I get the opportunity, I won't do it. Or I'll tell myself I'm going to do something romantic and continually put it off. She tells me I'm a good husband. But I know I could take our relationship to another level if I could just be more open about myself around her. But I just can't bring myself to do it because something about it scares me. I don't get it. I've parachuted from airplanes in the Army into a midnight sky but I can't sit face to face on the couch with a 5'3" woman and tell her how I feel.*

HOW THE HIDDEN LOVER CAN OPEN UP MORE

Obviously from the words of the hidden lover above, the first step for change in the hidden lover's life is opening up instead of shutting down. But this isn't just opening up to other people, it's first opening up to himself. So many times when a man is asked to talk about how he feels, he hasn't really sorted through it all himself. This is one of the reasons so many men don't want to talk about their feelings. Feelings are tough to get a grasp on, especially for men. Here are some specific steps he can use to help him establish a connection to his own feelings.

1. The hidden lover needs to listen to his heart.

The hidden lover needs to have a meeting with himself. It sounds simple and basic, but it's absolutely necessary. A man has to take the time to listen to his own thoughts, feelings and emotions, take time for personal reflection. The pressures and demands of life often make it difficult to do that. Often we intend to find some quiet time, but we don't get around to it. We push our personal time off in the interest of transacting more business. Or we consider personal time any time we're engaged in pleasurable activities such as watching a football game. But that's an activity, not the same as time for personal reflection. Personal reflection time is accomplished in surroundings that allow a man to hear himself think.

To do this, some guys meditate. Some like to go into natural surroundings to sit or walk. Most cities have plenty of quiet tucked-away places for meditation or reflective thinking. When I began to look for places to relax, I found parks, arboretums and nature preserves all around me that I didn't even know were there until I started looking for them. That's the first step. The next step is to make yourself take the time to go and relax, think or meditate. Some men find this hard to do because they have to be doing something, even to relax. If you're one of these guys, I hope you'll eventually learn to absolutely relax. But until that time, find a relaxing activity that has peaceful scenery. Fishing is a good example of relaxing because you're out in a natural setting. Jogging and hiking are also good ways to be engaged in an activity that will encourage peaceful creative thinking. Some good indoor activities for achieving a peaceful state of mind are listening to relaxing music, soaking in a comfortable tub or reading a good novel.

2. The hidden lover needs to listen to his woman.

I mentioned this before, but as with several topics in this book, it needs to be stated again. Another important step in the hidden lover learning to open himself up is listening to his significant other. One of the biggest complaints women have about men is that we don't listen. Or when we do listen, we tend to feel that our mate is asking us to solve a problem for her. I'm talking from experience here. I've had to learn to take a deep breath when my wife is talking about something that she is having trouble with. After the deep breath, I remind myself—just listen, don't try to fix it. Having success with this technique has only come with lots of practice. Practicing being a good listener can contribute immensely to a relationship because good listening develops empathy, a core element in strong relationships.

3. The hidden lover needs to practice expressing himself with words.

I'm reminded of what Sandy, a publishing industry executive, once said to me. When I told Sandy what I was writing this book about, she shared an anecdote about her husband. She recalled a time they were trying to resolve an issue between them; when she asked her husband about his feelings on the matter, his response was that of a computer, "Invalid question. File not found." I found that story very funny, but beyond the humor we men have to take it a step further.

Guys, we have to practice opening up, because it isn't something that comes easily for us. If you wanted to improve your jump shot, you'd get on the court and start shooting. If you wanted to lower your golf score, you'd take time to work on your drive, your putting, etc. The same goes for opening ourselves up! We have to work at it. No, it won't be easy. But remember, the reward of being able to open up is that it will make your life better. You'll carry less stress and feel that your significant other is an ally instead of someone you have to accommodate, only listen to, or do things for. When you feel that way, your relationship will shift to a new level of romance and intimacy.

Getting started on self-transformation is always the hard part. Men often ask me, Where do I start? Or what's something small I can do to start making the big changes? To paraphrase an old Asian proverb, "Every great journey begins with a single step." Therefore, in the next section, I'll speak directly to the hidden lovers reading this book on how they can make that first small step.

THE HIGH-FIVE FOR MEN: AN EASY PLACE TO BEGIN

1. Fight the "why bother" attitude.

Sometimes we guys feel so overloaded with work and day-to-day realities that we think the last thing we want is to go home and try to be more sensitive and open in our relationships. We fear it will be yet another drain on our already depleted energies for the day. So instead, we default to the "why bother" zone. That's a place where we rationalize, thinking: the bills are paid, there's a roof over our heads and we have food to eat; so why do I need to try to work on being sensitive. I'm doing my job! But, guys, fight that. That's one of the most convenient and popular excuses to close off. Having the essential things taken care of for your family is great, but that is a different task than developing your relationship with your wife/or girlfriend.

2. Fight the "lone warrior" mentality.

Being a man can be a very lonely proposition sometimes. This is because men tend to neglect building the intimate support systems necessary to provide us with emotional support and an outlet for our fears and concerns. Thus, the lone warrior mentality develops. This is a sort of self-pity men fall into because they feel isolated by the feeling that nobody understands them or can help them with their problems. But men don't have to suffer this way. Don't allow the lone warrior mentality to set in. Your wife or girlfriend is there to be part of the relief you need. She provides the feminine energy your spirit needs. Also, your male friends are there to empathize with you. Chances are, they're feeling like lone warriors too. Just last night I was feeling tinges of the lone warrior mentality creeping up on me so I called a friend. By the time I got off the phone I felt like a new man; and so did he because he said he needed to talk to another man too.

3. Learn what triggers you to close yourself off.

All men aren't the same when it comes to closing off. Something that makes me close myself off might not bother another guy, or vice versa. All of us have things we have no problems discussing as well as issues that are taboo to us. When you take time to identify when you feel yourself closing off because of something your wife/girlfriend is saying, you'll be in a better position to prevent yourself from shutting down, or at least be able to slow the conversation down until you are able to adjust to where it is going. Pay attention to how you feel when certain issues arise. Do you become tense, anxious or angry? If so, these are your trigger points to closing off.

4. Push yourself to discuss something you're "sitting" on.

You know how you push yourself in the gym to do just one

more curl or bench press? Well, that's the same way we have to approach issues we want or need to discuss with women. There is no easy way or trick to doing some things other than diving in. Sometimes it is that way with an issue you feel the need to bring into the open. Just think of it the way you think of anything else you do by forging ahead—such as a tough project at work, running the extra mile, or pushing yourself to go to school after working all day. Sometimes that's the kind of self-discipline and effort you have to put into making yourself bring issues out into the open with your wife/girlfriend.

5. Don't be so defensive in discussions.

In my previous book, *Understanding the Tin Man*, I mentioned this action and called it "raising the shield." It's very important for us men to learn to have discussions with our wives/girlfriends without being defensive, without raising our shields. Often we tend to feel blamed when our significant other brings up an issue. When we feel blamed, we shut down. Therefore, nothing gets accomplished and frustrations grow. The key is to learn to listen with objectivity— listen to what she is saying without preparing a defense before you've heard all of what she has to say. When you can accomplish that, you'll find that solutions and agreements will come more easily between you and your mate.

THINGS TO THINK ABOUT

1. What issues stand in the way of you and your mate experiencing greater intimacy in your relationship?
2. Are you willing to work on the issues that trigger emotional shut-downs?
3. Specifically, how can you and your mate provide mutual support to transform your lives and relationship?

JOURNAL ENTRY

What's your big issue or issues? What are the things you need courage to work on and face in your life? Write a break-free plan for yourself. Make it a point-by-point plan. Elaborate a little on each part of the plan. Include the tools you will need to make this plan work. For example, your plan may include improving your spiritual life, improving your health, lowering your stress level, ending an unhealthy association with someone, being more open in your relationship, etc. What steps will be involved? What people or professionals will you need to involve (i.e., doctor, therapist, clergy, etc.)? Don't limit yourself to the tools at your disposal. Instead, write down what you actually need. Then you can start working toward making it happen.

A LETTER FROM THE HIDDEN LOVER, PART 14

Now that I've read the book *The Hidden Lover*, I've done some soul-searching and I'm ready to take the next step toward leaving this part of myself behind.

The reason I wrote you all of these letters is that the book recommended writing about my feelings as a way to sort out and deal with things. The author said that when writing letters to our wives or girlfriends, it was up to each man whether or not to actually give the letters to his significant other. In my case there was no doubt that I'd give you these letters because within them are seeds for our love to grow.

I don't know what your reaction will be. I guess shock is the first reaction you'll have when I hand you all of these letters. You'll be surprised to find out that I was even reading a book like this. Ordinarily I wouldn't, but I heard this guy on the radio a few weeks ago and he sounded like a real down-to-earth man's man who was making good sense about how emotions and relationships are important to men. I even called in to ask him a question and he really hit on some things that I'd been thinking and feeling. It was good to have a chance to see that I wasn't alone in the things I was thinking and feeling because I've had some of these things bottled up for a long time.

Some of the things in my letters may come as a surprise to

you. I hope you're touched to know how deeply I feel for you. On the other hand, some of the things may cause you to get a little angry. But I hope not because I'm writing in the spirit of conciliation, not contention. Please read these letters with the love that was written into them.

But now comes my part. Now I've got to work on myself. I've got to do the follow-through. Reading the book just helped me prepare. So despite all I've said to you in the letters, now I've got to make the changes that I need to make. This is the hard part and I'm not sure how long it will take—years or maybe a lifetime. Maybe I won't be able to totally change some things, only modify them or smooth them out. I don't know. But I'm sure that I can stick with this idea of changing some things about myself because I clearly see the benefits. I can see that our relationship will grow stronger. I even see how it will help me become better in my professional life.

I used to fear not feeling in control of everything, especially my feelings. But now I've grown to realize that there's more power in letting go and letting God steer the controls. I already feel stronger just realizing that I can use my emotions as a muscle. Just like a biceps or triceps, my emotions are actually another source of strength for me. You'll be seeing a new man, albeit piece by piece. Please be patient with me and walk by my side through this process of change.

Love,
Your No Longer Hidden Lover

A SPECIAL MESSAGE

Thoughts on Remembering to Love

A few weeks after the tragedy of September 11, I read an article in the local paper that said divorce filings had slowed since 9/11. Shortly after that, I saw a special report on a network news show about how more people were deciding to get married since 9/11. For Americans, marriages were up, divorces were down and people who were together were finding ways to stay together.

In the midst of adversity, we rediscover the fundamental importance of our relationships. The part of our relationships that often gets hidden under the stresses of day-to-day living, the 9-to-5 shuffle, paying bills and the incessant drive to get one notch higher in society. Tragedy has a way of clearing all of that away from our minds and giving us new clarity.

Within that clarity we get a new view of our relationships. No longer is it such a big deal that he doesn't squeeze all of the toothpaste out of the tube or leaves the toilet seat up. No longer is it so important that she gained a few pounds over the years or wants you to dress up and go out for dinner and dancing. With surprising quickness, tragedy, or the threat of it, can transform things that once seemed to be problems into unimportant details or even endearing reminders of a person's presence in our lives.

I believe we are at an important time in our nation's history—indeed the history of the world. We're at a point where we have been forced to do a critical self-examination, resulting in a catharsis of our souls. So often it is the essential moments—birth, marriages and especially death—that serve to redefine our thinking. Like nothing else, the passing of a friend or relative pushes us into deep introspection of what our lives are about and how we conduct our lives, often causing us to make profound changes. As a nation, we experienced that type of profound change on 9/11. On that fateful day, we were shaken into a realization of all that we have to appreciate in the worst way, by having it savagely, though momentarily, taken from us.

In this self-examination, we've remembered that relationships form the foundation of our very lives. We've seen our relationships with new clarity. We've remembered what love really is and how profound a difference it makes in our lives. Let's hold on to that feeling. Let's remember love isn't a game merely for entertainment, and that other people and their feelings aren't expendable. To have someone to love is a blessing from God. Let's hold on to our loved ones, for they are with us only for a season.

WEB RESOURCES

Men's Issues

www.vix.com/menmag
Men's Voices Magazine: A general resource for information on men's issues

www.menshealthnetwork.org
Information clearinghouse for men's health issues

www.blackhealthnetwork.com
Information and articles on health issues for African Americans

www.preventchildabuse.org
Information about all forms of child abuse

www.nomsv.org
Information for male survivors of sexual abuse from the
National Organization on Male Sexual Victimization

www.niddk.nih.gov/health/urolog/urolog.htm
Information on urological diseases, impotence, etc., from
the National Institute of Diabetes and Digestive and Kidney
Diseases

www.fatherhood.org
Information and resources on fatherhood

www.themenscenter.com
Information clearinghouse for issues affecting men

www.webcrawler.com/relationships/advice/for_men
Relationship advice for men

AOL Keyword: Men
General topics about men

www.askmen.com
Topics about men and dating

Relationships and Marriage

AOL Keyword: Relationships
General relationship advice and information for couples

www.couples-place.com
General relationship advice and information for couples

www.ivillage.com/relationships
General relationship advice and information for couples

www.dir.yahoo.com/society_and_culture/relationships
General relationship advice and information for couples

www.about.com/people
General relationship advice and information for couples

www.love.msn.com
General relationship advice and information for couples

www.marriage.rutgers.edu
The National Marriage Project's web site with a variety of information on marriage

www.drruth.com
Questions and answers about sex

www.relationshipweb.com
General relationship advice and information for couples

www.sex-centre.com
The San Jose Marital and Sexuality Center's website featuring a variety of informative topics on sex

Therapists / Psychological Information

www.aamft.org
American Association for Marriage and Family Therapy website

www.abpsi.org
Associaton of Black Psychologists website

www.apa.org
American Psychological Association website

Christian / Spirituality Based Relationships

www.beliefnet.com
Multi-faith information source

www.christiananswers.net/sex/home.html
Issues in Christian romantic relationships

African-American Relationships

www.askheartbeat.com
Issues, articles and advice specifically on relationships
involving African Americans

www.blacklove.net
Issues, articles and advice specifically on relationships
involving African Americans

BOOKS TO HELP HIDDEN LOVERS HEAL AND WOMEN TO BETTER UNDERSTAND THEM

References are listed alphabetically by author.

John Bradshaw, *Men and Women Are from Earth After All* (Audio: Bradshaw Cassettes)

Barbara De Angelis, *What Women Want Men to Know* (Hyperion)

Walter De Milly, *In My Father's Arms: A True Story of Incest (Living Out)*, (University of Wisconsin Press)

Jed Diamond, *Surviving Male Menopause: A Guide for Women and Men* (Sourcebooks)

Bill and Pam Farrel, *Men Are Like Waffles—Women Are Like Spaghetti* (Harvest House)

Warren Farrell, *Women Can't Hear What Men Don't Say* (Tarcher/Putnam)

Warren Farrell, *Why Men Are the Way They Are* (Berkley)

Herb Goldberg, *What Men Really Want* (NAL)

Derek S. and Darlene Powell Hopson, *Friends, Lovers and Soul Mates* (Fireside)

Mic Hunter, *Abused Boys: The Neglected Victims of Sexual Abuse* (Fawcett)

Charles B. Inlander, the People's Medical Society, *Men's Health for Dummies* (Hungry Minds)

Ernest H. Johnson, *Brothers on the Mend* (Pocket)

William July II, *Brothers, Lust and Love* (Doubleday)

William July II, *Understanding the Tin Man* (Doubleday)

Mike Lew and Ellen Bass, *Victims No Longer: Men*

Recovering from Incest and Other Sexual Child Abuse (HarperCollins)

Terrence Real, *I Don't Want to Talk About It: Overcoming the Secret Legacy of Male Depression,* (Fireside)

James W. Reed, M.D., Neal Shulman, M.D., Charlene Shucker, *The Black Man's Guide to Good Health* (Hilton)

George Edmond Smith, *More Than Sex: Reinventing the Black Male Image* (Kensington)

Iyanla Vanzant, *Up from Here: Reclaiming the Male Spirit* (Harper San Francisco)

GROUP DISCUSSION TOPICS

The following topics are formatted for group discussions. Using the referenced chapter as a spark, host a discussion of men and women in your group, organization or community. I suggest trying a panel or moderated format for the discussion. If you try the panel style you should have no more than two men and two women on the panel to assure that each panelist will get ample time to speak and respond to questions. Basically you can take questions directly from the floor. Or if you want more control over the forum, you can ask audience members to write their questions on index cards and have the panelists select questions to respond to. You could also have a moderator select the questions and pass them to the panelists.

If you're in a lively group that wants a more free-flowing exchange, try the moderated style. In this form of discussion a moderator poses issues to the audience and allows audience members to get on the microphone with their answers to the questions posed. It's most fun when men pose questions to which women respond and vice versa. The questions can be taken live from the floor or written on index cards for the moderator to read. Just remember to remain civil and have fun. Don't get too emotional. The point is for both sexes to come away having had a positive experience.

1. Are you a hidden lover?

Do you have things affecting your relationship that you feel you can't discuss with your mate for some reason? Why do people sometimes feel they can't communicate openly with their mate? Is this a common issue for both men and women?

(Reference: Chapter 1, Real Lover or Hidden Lover: Which One Is He?)

2. Does a man have to be superman?

Many women say they don't expect men to play superman, but do they really mean it? What's the role of men today when it comes to earning income and handling responsibilities in a relationship or marriage?

(Reference: Chapter 4, How Trying to Be Superman Creates a Hidden Lover)

3. Why do men do a disappearing act?

What makes a man just up and walk out on a relationship with little or no explanation? Why do some guys start off a dating relationship hot and suddenly get cold? How do some men play phone games by trying to make a woman wait for their call?

(Reference: Chapter 2, How Hidden Lovers Hide in Relationships)

4. What makes a relationship feel like a ball and chain?

Are men overburdened in relationships with rules, regulations and expectations on their behavior? What makes a man feel like a relationship is a potential threat to his freedom and autonomy?

(Reference: Chapter 6, How Fear of Losing Freedom Affects the Hidden Lover)

5. How do hidden lovers really feel about sex?

Do the opinion polls, magazines, television and movies really tell the way most men feel about sex? How is he similar to the images of male sexuality in the media? How is he different?

(Reference: Chapter 8, The Hidden Lover's Views on Sex: He's Not Like All the Other Guys)

6. How can people work through emotional pain?

What are some emotionally painful events from a person's

past that can interfere with his or her ability to be intimate, both emotionally and sexually? What are some ways a couple can approach these issues constructively for a solution?

(Reference: Chapter 3, His Hidden Pain)

7. How can men and women better honor and respect each other in relationships?

How can a couple express honor and appreciation for each other? What are some specific things a couple can do for each other to maintain their level of respect for each other? How can they show appreciation for each other?

(Reference: Chapter 7, The Hidden Lover's Need for Appreciation and Respect)

8. How can men and women communicate more smoothly?

Are there things a man and woman in a relationship shouldn't talk about? What issues need special handling? How do you communicate a problem in the relationship to your mate without causing an argument? How do you communicate with someone who is highly emotional, or focused on logic?

(Reference: Chapter 9, Why the Hidden Lover Feels He Can't Really Talk to You)

9. Everything you wanted to know about the opposite sex but were afraid to ask.

This is an open-ended free-for-all discussion of uncensored questions and answers. Women should feel free to ask whatever they want to know about men and men should feel free to do the same about women. It's guaranteed fun.

(References: Chapter 13, Answers to Questions About Hidden Lovers, and Chapter 10, The Ladies Have Their Say)

10. How can couples avoid pitfalls in relationships?

How does a couple deal with obstacles they know they will face? How does a couple handle unexpected problems? How can a couple give their relationship regular checkups to avoid extra problems?

(Reference: Chapter 11, Hidden Relationship Sinkers)

11. How can a woman help a hidden lover change?

What boundaries should a woman draw with a man who is making changes in his life? What is defined as being supportive and what should be considered being a doormat? How do women make exits from relationships that won't work after trying to make them work?

(Reference: Chapter 12, Help, I'm in Love with a Hidden Lover! What You Can and Can't Do to Help Him)

WILLIAM JULY
ONLINE AND IN PERSON

The Hidden Lover *Online*

www.williamjuly.com

- Keep posted on media appearances, events, and tour information.

- Read William July's online advice column.

- Participate in research questionnaires and interviews for studies and new books.

- Read excerpts from William July's previous books—
    *Understanding the Tin Man: Why So Many Men
    Avoid Intimacy*
    *Brothers, Last and Love: Thoughts on Manhood, Sex
    and Romance.*

- Find out how to book William July for your event.

2/03